SEASONING LENT

40 Days of Recipes and Reflections

VOLUME 2 / YEAR B

Reflections by Stacy Smith

Recipes by Church Health Center Wellness

Church Health Center
Memphis, TN

About the Church Health Center
The Church Health Center seeks to reclaim the Church's biblical commitment to care for our bodies and our spirits. Long recognized as a national model for serving the uninsured, the Center has spent years connecting people of faith and their congregations with quality health resources and educational experiences. To learn more about the Center, visit ChurchHealthCenter.org. To learn more about our magazine on health ministry *Church Health Reader*, visit CHreader.org.

About Church Health Center Wellness
Church Health Center Wellness is the Center's Medical Fitness Facility that offers everything from personalized exercise plans and health education to activities for children and families. All the recipes in *Seasoning Lent* were developed by the staff of the Center's Wellness Education department for use in our Nutrition Kitchen, where we offer daily cooking classes for children, teens and adults.

About the Author
Rev. Stacy Smith is Manager of Faith Community Outreach at the Church Health Center and Parish Associate at Idlewild Presbyterian Church in Memphis, TN. She is the co-author of *Bless Her Heart: Life as a Young Clergy Woman* and author of several pieces for *Church Health Reader*.

Seasoning Lent: 40 Days of Recipes and Reflections, Volume 2 / Year B

© 2012 Church Health Center, Inc.
Memphis, TN

ISBN: 978-1-62144-000-0

Printed in the United States of America

Devotions by Stacy Smith
Recipes by Carolyn Nichols, Suzanne Ray, Esther Wills and the staff of Church Health Center Wellness Education
Edited by John Shorb, Stacy Smith, Sara Beth Taylor and Rachel Thompson
Layout and cover image by Lizy Heard and Rachel Thompson
Photography by Lizy Heard and Rachel Thompson

The primary objective of *Seasoning Lent* is to help your community incorporate healthy habits into their lives during the season of Lent. Please feel free to copy and distribute this resource to your congregation or community.

The Church Health Center welcomes your feedback. Please send your comments to FCO@churchhealthcenter.org.

Contents

Introduction

How do you observe the Christian season of Lent? Is Lent a yearly season that you are familiar with, or something you have never heard of? Do you have classic traditions that you keep each year, or do you struggle to commit to even the smallest of sacrifices? Does celebrating Lent seem like a chore or an opportunity? A chance to explore your Christian faith or just another seasonal resolution you have to keep? And how does the practice of Lent prepare you for a more joyful, more glorious Easter Sunday?

All of these are questions that we bring to this Lenten devotional, *Seasoning Lent*. For the next eight weeks, we invite you to explore an ancient Christian practice through a modern lens: cooking and eating special foods in the season of Lent.

For many Christians, the food we eat often has little to do with our faith. This is not true for many other faith traditions: many Jews refrain from eating pork or shellfish, Hindus are generally vegetarians, and devout Muslims routinely fast during the holy month of Ramadan. Yet Christians rarely engage in food sacrifice or fasting as an act of devotion or worship. For example, many Christians may be vegetarians, but usually the reasons for this practice are focused on the health of their body or the society in which they live. Rarely, do we as Christians change our eating habits because of religious reasons, and it can be difficult to see how what we eat affects our spiritual health and well-being.

The one exception is in Lent. This is traditionally a time when we practice sacrifice as a way of remembering Christ's sacrifice on the cross. It is a period of fasting, a time when we honor simplicity, sacrifice and spiritual growth. This fasting has both theological and physical roots. Traditionally, Lent comes at the very end of the season when the supplies from the harvest are gone, rotted or scarce. So fasting reminds us of the sacrifice offered by Christ, but it also forces us to sacrifice our immediate desires for the good of the whole. It helps us to learn spiritual lessons in our bodily home.

And for many Christians, food sacrifice is still a big part of their Lenten discipline. We may refrain from eating meat on Fridays, or eating meat at all, or cut out the usual temptations from our diet – chocolate, caffeine, or candy. In more recent years, however, even this act of devotion has begun to pass away. Some folks are more likely to "take up" a discipline in Lent rather than "give up" something they enjoy. While there is certainly nothing wrong with this practice, it doesn't always serve to remind us that the food we enjoy has a direct connection with our spiritual health and the health of our communities. Lent is a particularly good time to remind ourselves that our bodies and spirits are intimately connected, and paying special attention to the food we consume is especially important in Lent. It's historically, spiritually and practically rooted in our faith.

So for this season of Lent, we invite you on a journey of discipline that asks you to both "take up" and "give up." We will take up the practice of cooking and teach you new ways to create healthy, filling and tasty foods that feed both our bodies and our spirits. But we will also ask you to give up some of the more common ingredients and cooking practices that make our foods less healthy than they should be. We will enjoy the abundance of God's creation while taking seriously our responsibility to care for it. And we will practice new spiritual disciplines, just as generations of Christians have done during the season of Lent.

How to Use *Seasoning Lent*

The season of Lent begins on Ash Wednesday and lasts for the 40 days leading up to Easter Sunday. *Seasoning Lent* provides a weekly scriptural reflection and 40 recipes, one for each day in Lent. The first reflection is designed for the Sunday before Ash Wednesday, and each week's reflection sets the tone for the theme and recipes for each week. Each week then offers a different recipe that you can prepare as part of your devotional practice. We suggest that you read the Sunday reflections and use those days as a way to prepare for the recipes you will make throughout the week.

In addition to the daily recipes, each week offers practical ideas for how you can put *Seasoning Lent* into practice in your home and at church. If you are using *Seasoning Lent* as a personal devotional, each week gives you a new way to incorporate the Scriptural lessons into your daily life. And if several people in your church are using *Seasoning Lent*, each week offers ideas for programs in the church that can help support the community in their Lenten discipline. As you prepare for each week of *Seasoning Lent*, explore these tangible ways to successfully change your eating habits and enhance your spiritual practice.

A Note on Ingredients

Throughout *Seasoning Lent*, certain recipes will call for the following ingredients. Olive oil is used in many recipes because of its nutritional benefits. Some recipes call for extra-virgin olive oil, but you can interchange whatever kind of olive oil you have in your pantry. Some of these special ingredients can be somewhat pricey, or an ingredient might not be of use to you in future cooking. Instead of purchasing the ingredient from the store, see if someone in your church or neighborhood would be willing to share with you. If you have some of the below ingredients, you could share with them!

Herbs and spices

bay leaves
cayenne pepper
chili powder
cinnamon
crushed red pepper
    flakes
cumin
dried basil
dried oregano
dried parsley
dried rosemary
dried thyme
fresh ginger
garlic powder
ground coriander

ground flaxseed
nutmeg
onion powder
sage leaves
salt-free Cajun seasoning
tahini

Sauces, Oils, Vinegars

balsamic vinegar
olive oil
reduced-sodium soy
    sauce
sesame oil
vanilla extract

Dry goods

bread flour
brown sugar
cashew butter
cornmeal
chicken bouillon cube
dried cranberries
low-sugar strawberry
    preserves
Panko breadcrumbs
peanuts
pecans
pine nuts
red curry paste
walnuts

A Note on Cooking Utensils and Wares

As you begin *Seasoning Lent*, you might find that you do not have the cooking implements necessary for certain recipes. Many things can be substituted for other things, like using a fork instead of a whisk or in place of a potato masher. If you are missing something essential, see if someone in your church or in your neighborhood has one you could borrow. This could be a chance to cook with friends!

Cooking Utensils

Measuring spoons: 1 tablespoon, 1 teaspoon, ½ teaspoon, ¼ teaspoon and ⅛ teaspoon
Measuring cups: 1 cup, ½ cup, ⅓ cup, and ¼ cup
Whisk
Spoon
Fork
Knife
Cutting board
Can opener
Spatula
Wooden Spoon
Metal serving spoon
Spatula
Potato masher
Small Bowl
Medium bowl
Large bowl
microwavable plate
microwavable bowl
Blender or food processor
Cooking spray
Aluminum foil
Fine mesh strainer
Apple corer (optional)
Paper towels
Ladle

Cheese grater
Muffin tin liners
Tongs
Bread knife
Basting brush
Vegetable peeler
Zester

Pots, Pans and Baking Dishes

Small saucepan with lid
Medium saucepan with lid
Large saucepan with lid
Large skillet
Large stockpot
Baking dish (8x8 inch and 9x9 inch)
Muffin pan *or* ramekins
Small skillet
Roasting pan
Round pie pan (10 inch diameter)
Baking sheet
Dutch oven
Baking pan (15x10 inch)
Baking dish (13x9 inch)
Large cast iron skillet

Special Items

Grill or Grill pan
Food processor

Change: *What You Eat Matters*

MONDAY
Gouda Macaroni and Cheese

TUESDAY
The Best Chili

WEDNESDAY
Baked Pretzels

THURSDAY
Kale Chips

FRIDAY
Pumpkin Quesadillas with Cranberry Orange Salsa

SATURDAY
Steamed Broccoli

Gouda Macaroni
and Cheese
see page 12

Pumpkin Quesadillas with
Cranberry Orange Salsa
see page 16

Change: *What You Eat Matters*
Mark 9:2-10

And he was transfigured before them, and his clothes became dazzling white, such as no one on earth could bleach them.
—Mark 9: 2b-3

"Change comes from within." No one really knows who first uttered this famous phrase, but it could have come from Mark. In his telling of the transfiguration, Mark says that Jesus is transfigured in front of the disciples; in Greek, the word is *metamorphooai*, from which we get the word "metamorphosis." We tend to think that Jesus is the only person who is transfigured, that for this moment the "fully God" part was literally shining brighter than the "fully human" part. But Scripture tells us that other people are transfigured, too. Exodus 34 tells us that Moses' face shone as he descended from Mount Sinai, and in Acts 16, Stephen's "face shone like an angel." Paul even uses the same word *metamorphooai* to describe Christians: "And all of us...are being transformed into the same image from one degree of glory to another..." (2 Cor. 3:18) The Scriptures seem to say that in Christ, all of us are capable of transfiguration, and that we can all shine a gloriously divine light for all to see.

But living the transfigured life is not just something that happens. It begins within us. Jesus was transfigured in such a way that the glory of God shone from within Jesus himself. As pastor Warren Wiersbe says, "The word transfigured describes a change on the outside that comes from the inside. It is the opposite of 'masquerade,' which is an outward change that does not come from within. Jesus allowed his glory to radiate through his whole being."[1]

When it comes to our bodies and our health, we tend to have a "masquerade" point of view: if we change the outside, then somehow we will change the inside. But Jesus calls us to be a transfigured people, which works from the inside-out. We must be healthy on the inside in order to radiate health on the outside.

One way that we can become a transfigured people is to consider what we put within ourselves—literally, what we eat. When we eat food, we are able to make choices about what is within us. We have an opportunity and a responsibility to fill our insides with nourishment and energy. Unfortunately, these days, we also have the option of filling ourselves with junk. When we choose to fill ourselves with processed foods and harmful chemicals, we are living a healthy masquerade. The calling of transfiguration challenges us to think about how we are to live a healthy life from the inside-out.

This week, we will begin *Seasoning Lent* by living as a transfigured people. We will try to choose healthier options and fill ourselves with nourishing foods that help us to live healthier lives. By thinking differently about what we are putting within us, we will take the first step towards being a transfigured people.

Most loving God, be with us as we start this new Lenten journey. Just as you were transformed on the mountaintop, use our practice as a way of transforming the way we live. Show us new ways of being your children, in everything we do, say and eat. In Your holy name, Amen.

What to do:

▶ **At home:** Starting a Lenten practice like *Seasoning Lent* can be difficult. Inevitably, there will be times when we mess up a recipe or just don't have the energy to cook. But the point of a Lenten discipline is not to do things perfectly, but to try and live life a little differently. As you begin this new practice, think about what goals you have for your Lenten journey. Try to set smart goals for yourself that will stretch you—but not break you!

▶ **At church:** To help your congregation prepare for *Seasoning Lent,* have a "kitchen swap" at your church. Invite members to bring in extra kitchen items like measuring cups, mixing bowls or old blenders they rarely use and swap for items they need. A well-stocked kitchen will make the practice of cooking easier going forward.

Gouda Macaroni and Cheese

In Orthodox Christian traditions, the week before Lent begins is sometimes known as Cheesefare Week, a time when we enjoy the rich treats of butter and cheese before the start of Lent. Today we will prepare a version of macaroni and cheese as a way of honoring Cheesefare Week in a healthier way. Using low-fat ingredients minimizes the fat while spinach and whole-wheat ingredients boost the flavor and the nutritional value.

Prep Time: 10 minutes; **Total Time:** 35 minutes; **Makes 8 servings**
Serving Size: a little less than ¾ cup
Nutrition Facts (per serving): Calories: 200; Total Fat: 5 g; Sodium: 212 mg; Carbohydrate: 27 g; Fiber: 2 g; Protein: 10 g

Ingredients:

1 slice whole-wheat bread
1 tablespoon light butter
¼ cup thinly sliced green onions
2 garlic cloves, minced
2 tablespoons all-purpose flour
2 cups fat-free milk
½ teaspoon salt
¼ teaspoon black pepper
½ teaspoon onion powder

½ teaspoon garlic powder
½ cup (2 ounces) shredded smoked Gouda cheese
⅓ cup (about 1½ ounces) grated reduced-fat Parmesan cheese
5 cups coarsely chopped fresh spinach
4 cups hot, cooked, whole-wheat elbow macaroni (about 2 cups uncooked)
Cooking spray

Directions:

1. Preheat oven to 350 degrees. Place bread in a food processor, and pulse 10 times or until coarse crumbs measure ½ cup. Melt butter in a large saucepan over medium heat. Add green onions and garlic; cook 1 minute.
2. Add flour; cook 1 minute, stirring constantly. Gradually add milk, salt, pepper, onion powder and garlic powder, stirring constantly with a whisk until blended. Bring to a boil; cook until thick (about 2 minutes). Add cheeses; stir until melted. Add spinach and macaroni to cheese sauce, stirring until well blended. Spoon mixture into a 2-quart baking dish coated with cooking spray. Sprinkle with breadcrumbs. Bake at 350 degrees for 15 minutes or until bubbly.

The Best Chili

With roots similar to the tradition of Mardi Gras, Brazil is famous for its Carnaval, *a giant festival held before the beginning of Lent. Today we will make a simpler version of* feijoada, *considered by many to be a national dish of Brazil. This chili with black beans and ground turkey reminds us of the joyous revelry we associate with the day before the beginning of Lent.*

Prep time: 15 minutes; **Total time:** 50 minutes ; **Makes 10 servings**
Serving Size: 1 cup
Nutrition Facts (per serving): Calories: 209; Total Fat: 6 g; Saturated Fat: 2 g; Sodium: 260 mg; Carbohydrate: 25 g; Fiber: 8 g; Protein: 15 g

Ingredients:

1 pound ground turkey
1 tablespoon olive oil
1 yellow onion, chopped
1 green bell pepper, chopped
3 cloves garlic, chopped
1 cup frozen corn, thawed
1 teaspoon onion powder
1 teaspoon garlic powder
½ teaspoon salt

¼ teaspoon pepper
½ teaspoon cayenne pepper
2 tablespoons chili powder
15 ounces crushed tomatoes, no salt added
15 ounces tomato sauce, no salt added
½ cup water
1 can red beans, rinsed and drained
1 can black beans, rinsed and drained

Directions:

1. Preheat a large skillet to medium-high heat. Spray with cooking spray.
2. Add turkey and cook until no longer pink, about 6 minutes. Drain and set aside.
3. In a large, nonstick skillet, add olive oil. Once heated, add onion, pepper, garlic, corn and seasonings. Cook 6 minutes or until vegetables are softened.
4. Add remaining ingredients and cooked turkey and simmer for about 20-25 minutes.
5. Add more water if a thinner consistency is desired.

Baked Pretzels

The pretzel is a traditional food of Lent. This bread was made without the butter, milk or cheese that is traditionally forbidden in Lent. Perhaps more importantly, the shape of the pretzel is meant to remind us of arms crossed in prayer. On Ash Wednesday, we will make baked pretzels to honor the start of the season of Lent. If you like, you can omit the butter and salt as toppings in the last step to decrease the sodium.

Prep time: 10 minutes; **Total time:** 60 minutes for dough to rise, 30 minutes active time; **Makes 12 servings**
Serving Size: 1 pretzel
Nutrition Facts (per serving): Calories: 182; Total Fat: 2 g; Sodium: 359 mg; Carbohydrate: 35 g; Cholesterol: 5 mg; Fiber: 1 g; Protein: 5 g

Ingredients:

1 (.25 ounce) package active dry yeast
2 tablespoons brown sugar
1 teaspoon salt
1½ cup warm water
3 cups all-purpose flour
1 cup bread flour

2 cups warm water
2 tablespoons baking soda
2 tablespoons light butter, melted
1 teaspoon kosher salt
1 teaspoon onion powder or garlic powder

Directions:

1. In a large mixing bowl, dissolve the yeast, brown sugar and salt in the warm water. Stir in both flours. Form into a ball and knead dough on a floured surface until smooth, about 6 minutes. Place in a bowl with a light coating of olive oil.
2. Cover and let rise for 1 hour.
3. Preheat oven to 450 degrees. Combine 2 cups of warm water and baking soda in an 8-inch baking pan.
4. Cut dough into 12 pieces. Roll each piece into a 3-foot rope. Twist dough into a pretzel shape and dip in the baking soda and water.
5. Place pretzels on a cookie sheet lined with parchment paper. Let pretzels set for 15 minutes.
6. Bake for 10 minutes or until pretzels are golden brown. Brush pretzels with melted butter and sprinkle with salt and onion or garlic powder.

Kale Chips

As we begin Seasoning Lent, *you may not be used to cooking each day, or to using some of the cooking techniques that we will ask you practice. Today, we will prepare this easy dish to guide you into the practice of preparing daily meals. This would be a unique accompaniment to a sandwich or panini.*

Prep time: 10 minutes; **Total time:** 20 minutes; **Serves 6**
Serving size: about ½ cup
Nutrition Facts (per serving): Calories 37; Fat 3 g; Sodium 208 mg; Carbohydrates 3 g; Fiber 1 g; Protein 1 g

*Nutrition facts are based on 1 bunch of kale, 1 tablespoon olive oil and ½ teaspoon salt.

Ingredients:
1 bunch of kale
1 tablespoon olive oil

Variations (choose one):
½ teaspoon sea salt
2 tablespoons Parmesan cheese
1 tablespoon balsamic vinegar and ½ teaspoon sea salt (salt and vinegar chips)
½ teaspoon cinnamon, ½ teaspoon sugar, ½ teaspoon Splenda (kettle chips)
½ teaspoon sea salt and 1 teaspoon red pepper flakes

Directions:
1. Preheat oven to 350 degrees.
2. Wash and thoroughly dry kale. Tear into bite size pieces and place in a gallon size Ziploc bag.
3. Pour in 1 tablespoon of olive oil and shake until all pieces of kale are thoroughly coated.
4. Add your favorite seasoning from those listed above, and shake until evenly distributed.
5. Spread chips out on a foil lined cookie sheet and bake for 8-10 minutes. Edges should be brown, but not burned.

Pumpkin Quesadillas with Cranberry Orange Salsa

Today, we will prepare this meat-free dish to honor the Lenten traditions of refraining from meat on Fridays.

Prep Time: 10 minutes; **Total Time:** 35 minutes; **Makes 4 servings**
Serving Size: 1 quesadilla with salsa
Nutrition Facts (per serving): Calories: 242; Total Fat: 9 g; Saturated Fat: 2 g; Sodium: 163 mg; Carbohydrate: 35 g; Fiber: 5 g; Protein: 10 g

Ingredients for Quesadillas:

1 tablespoon vegetable oil
1½ cup pumpkin or winter squash, peeled, seeded, and cubed
1 medium onion, chopped
1 small red bell pepper, chopped
1 large tomato, chopped
½ cup cooked corn
½ teaspoon ground cumin
½ teaspoon ground coriander
½ teaspoon chili powder
Dash of salt

8 small corn tortillas
¾ cup Monterey Jack Cheese, low fat

Ingredients for Salsa:

1 navel orange and any other desired fruits for zest (strips of peeled citrus fruit skins)
¼ cup whole cranberries
2 tablespoons pecans
1 tablespoon granulated sugar substitute

Directions for Quesadillas:

1. Preheat oven to 450 degrees.
2. Heat oil in a large non-stick skillet over high heat. Add pumpkin and cook for 2 minutes, stirring often.
3. Add onions, peppers and cook for an additional 2 minutes.
4. Stir in tomatoes, corn and spices, cook for 2 minutes.
5. Transfer vegetables to a foil-lined cookie sheet and roast in oven for 8-10 minutes or until pumpkin is tender when pierced with a fork.
6. Heat a large skillet over medium heat and spray with cooking spray.
7. Add 1 tortilla, sprinkling with cheese, top with ¼ cup of pumpkin mixture made above. Again sprinkle with cheese and top with second quesadilla.
8. Flip tortilla after 45 seconds and heat other side. Repeat for other quesadillas.

Directions for Salsa:

1. Zest 1 orange by passing through a food processor or by using a paring knife to cut peel into thin strips.
2. Mix remaining chopped orange, cranberries, and pecans in a medium bowl. Blend until chucky, do not puree.
3. Sprinkle zested peels onto salsa.
4. Serve salsa (about 2 tablespoons per quesadilla) over warm quesadillas.

Steamed Broccoli

Steaming foods is an excellent cooking practice, and broccoli is packed with nutritional value and is linked to cancer prevention. It is easy to do and a particularly good way of preparing vegetables so they retain their nutritional value. Today we will prepare steamed broccoli as an easy Saturday dish.

Total Time: 7 minutes; **Makes 10 servings**
Serving Size: ½ cup
Nutrition Facts (per serving): Calories: 15; Total Fat: 0g; Sodium: 15 mg; Carbohydrates: 3g; Fiber: 1g; Protein: 1 g

Ingredients:
1 pound raw broccoli
¼ cup water
1 tablespoon lemon juice
lemon wedge for serving

Directions:
1. Place stems in a steamer basket over 2 inches of water (with 1 tablespoon lemon juice added to it) in a large pot set over high heat.
2. Cover and steam for 2 minutes. Add florets; cover and continue steaming until tender, about 3 minutes more. Sprinkle with lemon juice before serving.

Water: *What You Drink Matters*

MONDAY
White Bean Soup

TUESDAY
Braised Asparagus

WEDNESDAY
Stuffed Apples

THURSDAY
Spicy Thai Coconut Shrimp

FRIDAY
Penne Pasta with Spinach

SATURDAY
Poppy Seed Chicken Casserole

**Spicy Thai
Coconut Shrimp**
page 25

Stuffed Apples
see page 24

Water: *What You Drink Matters*

Mark 1:9-11

In those days Jesus came from Nazareth of Galilee and was baptized by John in the Jordan.
    —Mark 1:9

In the very beginning, God parts the waters to create the world. Moses leads the Israelites across the Red Sea and draws water from a rock in the wilderness. Isaiah tells us that the waters will not consume us, and John says that Jesus is the Living Water. And, perhaps most memorably, Jesus himself is baptized.

In Scripture, and in our world, water is the source of life. The Living Water of Christ can quench our souls and restore us to health. Baptism cleanses us of sin and brings us into the fullness of faith. And in our society, potable water is in great need. Perhaps never before has clean drinking water been so important to our health and the heath of our world. Water is central to our life, both physically and spiritually. Water brings us into the Christian life and sustains us in our physical life.

Yet it can often seem like the promise of the baptismal waters are very far from us. Wendell Berry, the writer and environmental leader, draws on experiences from his Kentucky farm and often speaks about the wonders of creation alongside the threats facing it. In his poem, simply entitled "Water," Berry speaks directly to these experiences of longing for and living without such vital waters:

> *I was born in a drought year. That summer*
> *my mother waited in the house, enclosed*
> *in the sun and the dry ceaseless wind,*
> *for the men to come back in the evenings,*
> *bringing water from a distant spring...*
> *I love the water of wells and springs*
> *and the taste of roofs in the water of cisterns.*
> *I am a dry man whose thirst is praise*
> *of clouds, and whose mind is something of a cup.*

My sweetness is to wake in the night
after days of dry heat, hearing the rain.[2]

Many of us live in a "drought year," both spiritually and physically. We thirst for the Living Water of Christ, but we also thirst for water itself. We walk around perpetually dehydrated. Whether we are thirsting for God or thirsting for health —or both—too many of us do not consume enough water. Water is the source of life and death. Without it, our bodies and our spirits can dry up and become brittle and weak. We need the Living Water of Christ and the physical water of life to keep us nourished, refreshed and whole.

This week we will focus on the importance of water. We will use water to prepare food and keep it moist and delicious. And of course, we remind you to drink plenty of water! Rather than living in the drought, this week we invite you to drink from the waters of life, and to drink of the Living Water.

God of the waters, quench our thirsts with your nourishing love. Reach into our parchedness and our drought-living and give us Your healing waters. Just as you blessed Jesus in the waters of the Jordan, pour your healing waters over us and let justice rain down. Help us to remember those whose thirsts are not quenched, who struggle for access to clean water, and give us strength to be living waters for others. In Your holy name, Amen.

What to do

▶ **At home:** What are some practical ways you can cut back on your household water consumption? Many of us routinely shut off the faucet while brushing our teeth, but there are other simple ways to avoid water waste, especially in the kitchen. This week, try to avoid defrosting food using running water and instead defrost in the refrigerator. Or soak pots and pans instead of letting the water run while you scrape them clean. Try to implement small ways of saving water in the kitchen, which will add up in the long run. For more ideas, visit www.wateruseitwisely.com.

▶ **At church:** Many churches and church denominations support programs that provide safe drinking water to people who have no access to it. Church World Service's Water for All enables access to potable water through local and global partnerships and supports community-based water projects. If your church is not involved in a water mission, begin the discussion with a special focus on water in worship and encourage your congregation to learn more about the Church's mission work around water access.

White Bean Soup

This wintry soup offers great flavor without a lot of fat or sodium. Pay attention to consistency of the bean puree—adding water allows you adjust the consistency to your taste. Enjoy this low-sodium soup with a green salad and some whole-wheat toast for a low-fat meal.

Prep time: 15 minutes; **Total time:** 30 minutes; **Makes 10 cups**
Serving Size: 1 cup
Nutrition Facts (per serving): Calories: 160; Total Fat: 2 g; Sodium: 27 mg; Carbohydrate: 28 g; Fiber: 7 g; Protein: 9 g

Ingredients:

3½ cups water
3 cans white beans, rinsed and drained
1 medium yellow onion, chopped
4 carrots, chopped
3 large tomatoes, chopped
4 cloves garlic, finely chopped

1 teaspoon dried thyme
½ teaspoon dried basil
1 teaspoon onion powder
1 teaspoon garlic powder
1 tablespoon olive oil
Salt and pepper to taste if desired

Directions:

1. Bring 3½ cups of water to a boil.
2. Puree half of the beans, adding a little water if necessary.
3. In a large saucepan or stockpot, heat olive oil and sauté garlic. Add the carrots and onion and sauté for 5 minutes or until tender.
4. Stir in tomatoes, basil and thyme. Cook an additional 5 minutes. Add water, bean puree and remaining beans. Season with onion powder, garlic powder, salt and pepper to taste. Simmer for 10-15 minutes.

Braised Asparagus

This simple dish will become a family favorite. Asparagus is rich in folic acid and is a good source of potassium, fiber, and other vitamins. Braising uses moist heat to cook the asparagus—a new way to think about cooking vegetables.

Prep Time: 2 minutes; **Total Time:** 7 minutes; **Makes 4 servings**
Serving Size: 1 cup (about 6-8 stalks)
Nutrition Facts (per serving): Calories: 54; Total Fat: 3 g; Sodium: 3 mg; Carbohydrates: 5 g; Fiber: 3 g; Protein: 0 g

Ingredients:
1 pound raw asparagus
Lemon, sliced
2 teaspoons olive oil
½ cup water

Directions:
1. Trim ends of asparagus by snapping the stalk or cut with a knife about 2 inches from the bottom of the stalk.
2. Place large skillet over high heat. Add ½ cup water, asparagus, and slice of lemon.
3. Cover, bring to a simmer and cook for about 5 minutes.

Stuffed Apples

This flavorful treat is great as a side dish or a dessert! The spices infuse these apples with a beautiful flavor. The secret to these apples is the water—putting a small amount of water in the bottom of the pan subtly steams the apples, making them soft and moist.

Prep time: 15 minutes; **Total time:** 45 minutes ; **Makes 8 stuffed apples**
Serving Size: 1 stuffed apple
Nutrition Facts (per serving): Calories: 121; Total Fat: 4 g; Sodium: 77 mg; Carbohydrate: 22 g; Fiber: 3 g; Protein: 1 g

Ingredients:

8 small apples
Lemon, cut in half
2 tablespoons light butter
2 tablespoons dark brown sugar
½ cup quick cooking oats
2 tablespoons golden raisins

2 tablespoons chopped walnuts
2 teaspoons ground cinnamon
¼ teaspoon ground nutmeg
Dash of salt
Water

Directions:

1. Preheat oven to 375 degrees. Spray a large baking dish with cooking spray.
2. Remove the core and seeds of each apple, but do not core all the way to the bottom of the apple. Squeeze lemon juice over each cored apple to prevent browning.
3. Place apples in the dish, with the cored area facing up.
4. Combine butter, dark brown sugar, oats, raisins, walnuts, cinnamon, nutmeg and salt in a large bowl. Stuff apples evenly with mixture. Sprinkle apples with additional cinnamon if desired.
5. Pour ¼ inch of water in the bottom of the baking dish. Bake in preheated oven for 35 minutes or until apples are soft.

Spicy Thai Coconut Shrimp

Time for Thai! Rethink your standard dinner cuisine with this fresh, tasty take on Thai food. Bell peppers, fresh asparagus and lean shrimp satisfy in this quick, healthy meal. Simply adjust the red curry paste to turn down the heat. This dish is filling on it's own, but if you're cooking for a crowd add a small side salad with a healthy vinaigrette dressing.

Prep Time: 10 minutes; **Total Time:** 25 minutes; **Makes 8 servings**
Serving Size: 1½ cups
Nutrition Facts (per serving): Calories: 346; Total Fat: 8.5 g; Saturated Fat: 4 g; Sodium: 187 mg; Carbohydrate: 39 g; Fiber: 2 g; Protein: 26 g; Calcium: 85 mg

Ingredients:

2 cups uncooked brown rice
2 tablespoons water
1 tablespoon red curry paste
2 pounds large raw shrimp, peeled and deveined
Cooking spray

1 pound asparagus, trimmed and sliced into 1-inch pieces
1 red bell pepper, sliced thin
1 cup green onions, chopped
Dash of salt
14 ounces canned light coconut milk

Directions:

1. Cook the rice according to the package directions, omitting any salt and fat additions.
2. While rice is cooking, combine the water and curry paste in a medium sized bowl. Add the shrimp to coat.
3. Place a large skillet coated with cooking spray over medium high heat. Add asparagus, bell peppers and green onions. Cover and cook for about 4 minutes. Add shrimp and cook for about 3 minutes. Stir in salt and coconut milk. Cook for an additional 4 minutes. Serve over rice.

Penne Pasta with Spinach

Olive oil and Parmesan cheese replace rich creamy sauces in this fresh take on penne pasta. Spinach and tomatoes are the perfect complement to the savory flavors of this easy entrée. Pair this dish with a small salad and fresh vinaigrette for a complete meal.

Prep time: 15 minutes; **Total Time:** 30 minutes; **Makes 8 servings**
Serving Size: 1½ cups
Nutrition Facts (per serving): Calories: 313; Total Fat: 10 g; Sodium: 182 mg; Carbohydrate: 50 g; Fiber: 12 g; Protein: 11 g

Ingredients:

8 cups cooked penne pasta
40 ounces frozen spinach, thawed, rinsed and squeezed of excess moisture
4 cloves garlic, chopped
4 tablespoons olive oil, divided

1 ounce Parmesan cheese, shredded
Dash of salt
Black pepper to taste
6 tomatoes, chopped

Directions:

1. Cook penne pasta according to package directions.
2. Heat 2 tablespoons of oil in a large skillet over medium-high heat. Add spinach, garlic and Parmesan cheese, and cook for 5 minutes.
3. Stir in tomatoes and cook an additional 3 minutes. Add salt and pepper.
4. Toss pasta into spinach mixture and add the remaining 2 tablespoons of olive oil. Serve warm.

Poppy Seed Chicken Casserole

This classic dish gets a healthful makeover by decreasing the fat and sodium content of the usual ingredients. Adding onion, celery and mushrooms boosts the flavor and adds fiber and nutrients. Once you taste this dish, you won't go back to your old recipe!

Prep Time: 15 minutes; **Total Time:** 60 minutes; **Makes 12 servings**
Serving Size: 1 cup
Nutrition Facts (per serving): Calories: 195; Total Fat: 10 g; Saturated Fat: 4 g; Sodium: 204 mg; Cholesterol: 43 g; Carbohydrate: 13 g; Fiber: 2 g; Protein: 14 g

Ingredients:

10 cups of water
3 raw, boneless, skinless chicken breasts
1 tablespoon olive oil
1 cup onion, chopped
½ cup celery, chopped
2 cups fresh mushrooms, chopped
3 cloves garlic, chopped
1 teaspoon garlic powder
1 teaspoon onion powder
½ teaspoon freshly ground black pepper
1 (8 ounce) can fat-free cream of mushroom soup
8 ounces fat-free sour cream
1 cup crushed whole-wheat, low-sodium crackers
1 tablespoon poppy seeds
½ cup light butter, melted

Directions:

1. Preheat oven to 350 degrees.
2. To cook chicken, bring 10 cups of water to a boil in a large stockpot. Add chicken breasts and boil until chicken is no longer pink, about 12 minutes. Once chicken is cooked, drain and let cool for 2 minutes. Cut chicken into 1-inch chunks.
3. Heat a large skillet to medium high heat, add olive oil. Swirl olive oil around the pan. Place onion, celery, mushrooms and garlic in pan. Cook for 5 minutes or until vegetables are tender. Season vegetables with onion powder, garlic powder and pepper.
4. Take mixture off the heat.
5. Place cooked chopped chicken in a large bowl; add the onion mixture along with the soup, sour cream and poppy seeds.
6. Place this mixture in a 9x13 inch glass baking dish coated with cooking spray.
7. In a small bowl, combine the crushed crackers and the melted butter, blend well. Sprinkle the buttered crushed crackers over the chicken mixture.
8. Bake in the preheated oven for 30 minutes or until casserole is brown and bubbly.

Sacrifice: *Making the Most of our Resources*

MONDAY
Spicy Tomato Soup

TUESDAY
Oven-Fried Chicken

WEDNESDAY
Lemon Green Beans

THURSDAY
Carrot Soufflé

FRIDAY
Mediterranean Roasted Broccoli and Tomatoes

SATURDAY
Tilapia in a Bag

Lemon Green Beans
see page 34

Mediterranean Roasted
Broccoli and Tomatoes
see page 36

WEEK 3

Sacrifice: *Making the Most of our Resources*

Mark 8:31-38

He called the crowd with his disciples, and said to them, "If any want to become my followers, let them deny themselves and take up their cross and follow me.
—Mark 8:34

In April of 1942, grocers in the United States stopped selling sugar. They resumed sales one week later after the War Ration Book Number One, known as the "Sugar Book," was distributed to citizens around the country. In addition to tires, coffee, penicillin, and a host of other items, sugar was rationed as a way of supporting the country's efforts in World War II. Each person could receive a half-pound of sugar per week—half the normal consumption for the time.

Some of us will remember the ration books, but many will not know of a time when we were asked to sacrifice something as common as sugar for a greater good. Yet as Christians, this is one of the most important practices of our faith. In Mark, Jesus calls us to deny ourselves and to follow him. One of the ways we can do this is by denying ourselves food, or fasting.

Fasting, or willingly abstaining from eating or drinking for a period of time, is very common throughout Scripture and is done for many different reasons. Moses, Samuel, Elijah, and Jesus all fast for different purposes—to mourn, to prepare, to repent, to demonstrate devotion. Fasting is similar to the sacraments: it is a physical manifestation of a spiritual commitment. It helps us learn spiritual lessons in our bodily home.

However, the Bible also clearly tells us that when fasting is divorced from justice, its efforts soon fall flat. Zechariah says very plainly in chapter 7 that pious fasting without concern for the widow, the orphan, the alien and the poor, will incur wrath from God. In chapter 58, Isaiah also offers his rebuke to those who would fast without justice in their hearts: "Why do we fast, but you do not see?... Look, you serve your own interest on your fast-day, and oppress all your workers. Look, you fast only to quarrel and to fight and to strike with a wicked fist...Is not this the fast that I choose: to loose the bonds of injustice, to undo the thongs of the yoke, to let the oppressed go free, and to break every yoke?" We are called to fast for justice, not just for ourselves.

This week we will practice "doing-more-with-less" and focus on the sacrifices we can make in our food choices. Rather than making a new meal each day, we will create a main dish and complement it with different sides. By focusing on the minimum amount we need, we can prepare ourselves for the sacrifices we are called to as Christians.

Merciful God, we hesitate to deny ourselves even the simplest of luxuries. Remind us that we are called to take up your cross and that we are capable of making sacrifices that support the common good. Help us to adjust our expectations and to enjoy the satisfaction of simply following in your ways. In Your holy name, Amen.

What to do:

▶ **At home:** The Bible has much to say about the reasons why people fast. This week, focus on biblical examples of fasting. Why are these people fasting, and what do they accomplish with their fast? Select two chapters from this list and compare their approach to fasting: Exodus 34, 1 Samuel 7, 1 Kings 19, Nehemiah 1, Jonah 3, Joel 2, Isaiah 58, Matthew 4, Luke 2, and Acts 13.

▶ **At church:** How would a fast work for your community? This week, explore the different ways that you can start or enhance the practice of fasting at your church. There are many different ways of fasting, depending on your tradition and health needs. Some churches fast together to draw attention to a cause or issue, or simply provide healthy hints for how people with different health challenges can safely fast. Challenge your community to think about how you might safely step outside your comfort zone and enhance your fasting practice.

Spicy Tomato Soup

Complex flavors and a light kick will leave you toasty with this simple soup. Enjoy it with some whole-grain toast drizzled lightly with olive oil for a simple but satisfying meal.

Prep time: 15 minutes; **Total time:** 35 minutes; **Makes 4 servings**
Serving Size: 1 cup
Nutrition Facts (per serving): Calories: 136; Total Fat: 3.5 g; Saturated Fat: 1 g; Sodium: 215 mg; Carbohydrate: 22 g; Cholesterol: 0 mg; Fiber: 5 g; Protein: 5 g

Ingredients:

1 (16 ounce) package frozen mixed bell pepper strips
1 (14.5 ounce) can no-salt-added diced tomatoes
1 (14.5 ounce) can fat free low-sodium chicken broth
1 (15.5 ounce) can no-salt-added navy beans, rinsed and drained
2 cloves garlic, chopped
¼ teaspoon crushed red pepper
1 tablespoon dried basil leaves
1 teaspoon dried parsley
1 teaspoon each onion powder and garlic powder
1 tablespoon balsamic vinegar
1 tablespoon olive oil
Dash of salt
½ teaspoon dried oregano

Directions:

1. In a food processor or blender, puree bell peppers, tomatoes, broth, beans, parsley, vinegar, oregano, garlic, crushed red pepper, garlic powder and onion powder until slightly chucky.
2. Pour mixture into a large saucepan and bring to a boil over high heat.
3. Reduce heat and simmer, cover for 20 minutes or until flavors are blended. Remove from heat, stir in salt and oil.

Oven-Fried Chicken

Fried chicken gets a healthy makeover. We've fixed up this Southern staple to reduce fat and bump up the flavor. You won't miss deep-fried chicken after trying this healthier alternative—the crisp, slightly spicy breading keeps the chicken tender and juicy. Serve with a whole-grain roll and a simple vegetable for a filling meal.

Prep Time: 10 minutes; **Total Time:** 30 minutes; **Makes 6 servings**
Serving Size: 1 chicken breast
Nutrition Facts (per serving): Calories: 225; Total Fat: 2 g; Saturated Fat: 1 g; Sodium: 275 mg; Carbohydrate: 22 g; Fiber: 1 g; Protein: 30 g

Ingredients:

½ cup cornmeal
½ cup Panko breadcrumbs
1 teaspoon dried tarragon
1 teaspoon dried basil
1 teaspoon dried oregano
¼ teaspoon salt
¼ teaspoon ground black pepper
¼ teaspoon ground red pepper

1 teaspoon onion powder
1 teaspoon garlic powder
4 egg whites
¼ cup low-fat buttermilk
½ cup white whole-wheat flour, sifted
6 4-ounce boneless, skinless chicken breasts
Cooking spray

Directions:

1. Preheat the oven to 375 degrees.
2. In a shallow pan, combine the cornmeal, breadcrumbs, tarragon, basil, oregano, salt, black pepper, red pepper, onion powder and garlic powder.
3. In another shallow pan, combine the egg whites and buttermilk.
4. In a third shallow pan, place the flour.
5. Coat the chicken with the flour, dip in egg mixture, then roll in cornmeal mixture.
6. Place in a large glass baking dish coated with cooking spray.
7. Bake uncovered for 18 minutes or until chicken is no longer pink in center and juices run clear.

Lemon Green Beans

Lemon, garlic and light butter do all the work in this simple side dish. Feel free to add different herbs as the seasons change. Keep this one in your recipe book—it's a healthy complement to almost any entrée!

Prep Time: 10 minutes; **Total Time:** 20 minutes; **Makes 4 servings**
Serving Size: ½ cup
Nutrition Facts (per serving): Calories: 53; Total Fat: 4 g; Saturated Fat: 1 g; Sodium: 152 mg; Carbohydrate: 4 g; Fiber: 2 g; Protein: 1 g

Ingredients:

1 tablespoon light unsalted butter
½ tablespoon olive oil
1 garlic clove, halved
2 cups green beans, washed and trimmed
1 teaspoon lemon zest
½ teaspoon oregano
½ teaspoon dried parsley
¼ teaspoon salt
½ teaspoon black pepper

Directions:

1. Melt butter, olive oil and garlic together on low heat for about 2 minutes. Remove from heat and allow garlic to sit in butter mixture for about five minutes.
2. While waiting for butter and garlic, bring a large pot of water to a boil. Once boiling, add washed and trimmed green beans. Boil until slightly tender, about 5 minutes.
3. Drain beans and quickly rinse under cold water for only a few seconds (this helps to stops the cooking process and keeps them nice and green!)
4. Remove garlic from butter mixture and toss green beans in the garlic-infused butter.
5. Add lemon zest, oregano, parsley, salt and pepper. Toss to coat.

Carrot Soufflé

Simple and sweet, this healthier take on carrot soufflé is low in fat but packed with wintry flavors. If you like, after baking, sprinkle the top of the casserole with cinnamon to add simple elegance.

Prep Time: 10 minutes**; Total Time:** 40 minutes**; Makes 8 servings**
Serving Size: ½ cup
Nutrition Facts (per serving): Calories: 114; Total Fat: 2 g; Saturated Fat: 1 g; Sodium: 239 mg; Carbohydrate: 20 g; Fiber: 1 g; Protein: 4 g

Ingredients:

3 cups sliced carrots
1 tablespoon light butter
2 eggs
4 egg whites
½ cup sugar
½ cup sugar substitute

⅓ cup skim milk
½ teaspoon salt
1 teaspoon ground cinnamon
½ teaspoon ground nutmeg
1 teaspoon vanilla extract

Directions:

1. Preheat oven to 350 degrees. Spray a 9x13 inch glass baking dish with cooking spray, set aside.
2. Place carrots and enough water to cover in a saucepan. Bring to a boil and let cook for about 20 minutes. Drain and cool carrots. Puree carrots to a smooth consistency in a food processor or blender.
3. In a medium bowl, mix the carrots, butter and remaining ingredients.
4. Spread mixture into the prepared casserole dish.
5. Bake for 30 minutes.

Mediterranean Roasted Tomatoes and Broccoli

Broccoli and tomatoes are some of the most flexible vegetables and can be prepared in many different ways. This recipe roasts the broccoli and tomatoes with garlic and olive oil for a delightful treat with added health benefit. Broccoli and tomatoes are consistently ranked as good to foods to fight cancer. Both add fiber and are also rich sources of nutrients.

Prep Time: 10 minutes; **Total Time:** 20 minutes; **Makes 4 servings**
Serving Size: about 1 cup
Nutrition Facts (per serving): Calories: 82; Total Fat: 5 g; Sodium: 275 mg; Carbohydrate: 6 g; Fiber: 4 g; Protein: 3 g

Ingredients:

12 ounces (about 4 cups) broccoli crowns, trimmed and cut into bite-size florets
1 cup grape tomatoes
1 tablespoon extra-virgin olive oil
2 cloves garlic, minced
¼ teaspoon salt

½ teaspoon freshly grated lemon zest
1 tablespoon lemon juice (about half a lemon)
10 pitted black olives
1 teaspoon dried oregano (or Italian herb blend)

Directions:

1. Preheat oven to 450 degrees.
2. Toss broccoli, tomatoes, oil, garlic and salt in a large bowl until evenly coated. Spread in an even layer on a baking sheet. Bake about 10 to 13 minutes, until the broccoli begins to brown.
3. Meanwhile, combine lemon zest and juice, olives, and oregano in a large bowl. Add the roasted vegetables; stir to combine. Serve warm.

Tilapia in a Bag

This fearless seafood recipe will bring healthy and delicious tilapia fish to your weekly table with minimal effort and infinite delight. Tilapia filets and whatever vegetables look most appealing to you at the market this week are placed in a parchment packet and seasoned with bright lemon, salt and pepper. This meal is great for individuals or families—each person can customize their entrée!

Prep Time: 10 Minutes; **Total Time:** 20 Minutes; **Makes 1 fillet with vegetables**
Serving Size: 1 fillet
Nutrition Facts (per serving): Calories: 180; Total Fat: 6.5 g; Saturated Fat: 1.5 g; Sodium: 124 mg; Carbohydrate: 8 g; Fiber: 2.5 g; Protein: 23 g

Ingredients:

1 (4-ounce) tilapia fillet
1 cup sliced vegetables of your choice (low-calorie vegetables such as broccoli, peppers, leeks, onions, carrots, etc.)
1 teaspoon extra-virgin olive oil

2 teaspoons lemon juice
1 teaspoon lemon zest
Salt and pepper to taste
1 sheet parchment paper

Directions:

1. Preheat oven to 400 degrees.
2. Place parchment paper on a large cookie sheet. Cut paper into a half heart. Place vegetables in center of paper. Place fish on top.
3. Drizzle lemon juice, oil and zest on top of fish. Season with salt and pepper if desired.
4. Seal bag and place in oven for 10 minutes or until fish flakes easily with a fork and vegetables are tender.

WEEK 4
Value: *Cost vs. Quality*

MONDAY
*Cauliflower Soup with
Carrots and Leeks*

TUESDAY
*Penne Pasta with
Pumpkin and Sausage*

WEDNESDAY
*Strawberry and Cream
Cheese Muffins*

THURSDAY
Mexican Lasagna

FRIDAY
White Bean Dip

SATURDAY
*Spaghetti Squash with
Kale and Chickpeas*

**Strawberry and Cream
Cheese Muffins**
see page 44

**Spaghetti Squash with
Kale and Chickpeas**
see page 47

Value: *Cost vs. Quality*

John 2:13-16

Making a whip of cords, he drove all of them out of the temple, both the sheep and the cattle. He also poured out the coins of the money changers and overturned their tables.
—John 2:15

Money-changing was big business in the ancient world, just as it is today. It's unclear from this Gospel account whether Jesus was against all business transactions in the Temple or just the unjust ones. Yet we do know that the business of money-changing and animal sacrifice was a boost for a few at the expense of many. We can surmise that if the money-changers had been conducting their business honestly, Jesus' response would probably have been less violent. As it was, those buying animals in the Temple were forced to pay prices that were much higher than the value of the product.

Looking at the news about the costs of different foods today, we might notice a similar situation. Many of us find ourselves paying a high cost for a low quality product. This "high cost" may be financial: one researcher suggests that while a meal for four at McDonald's is $28, a dinner of roast chicken and vegetables is only $14, which contradicts the commonly-held belief that fast food is cheaper than healthy food.[3] But even if fast food costs less, we still find ourselves paying a much higher cost for the unhealthy food we buy. When our diet consists of cheap, unhealthy food, we must remember that we will probably have to pay for our choices, one way or another, in the future. We may pay financially, spiritually, physically, or emotionally, but we are always making a sound investment when we choose the healthiest option rather than the cheapest one.

When it comes to eating healthy, perhaps we are asking the wrong question. Instead of asking "Which is cheaper?" we need to ask, "Which has the most value?" Rather than focusing strictly on the numbers, we could choose to focus on which experience is better for us, both immediately and in the long run. When we cook a healthy meal, we learn many valuable lessons. We learn about our tastes, our abilities, and our limitations. We engage our minds by calculating the exact amount of an ingredient to add, and we engage our hearts when we make something we truly love. And of course, in the long run, eating healthy will not only help us save money on health care costs. It will give us more opportunities to enjoy the things we love.

This week we will focus on preparing healthy meals that are cost-effective and of a high value. Just as Jesus brought down the money-changers, we too can change the course of our lives by choosing to eat foods of value.

God in the Temple, help us to keep our focus on things that are valuable instead of things that are cheap. Show us the value in attempting and completing the task of preparing the foods you have created in a creative, appealing and healthy way. When it is warranted, give us a righteous anger and the ability to stand up to injustice in whatever form it takes. And be with those who are taken advantage of, giving them power and vision to live in your love. In Your holy name, Amen.

What to do:

▶ **At home:** Do you have a food budget? Many of us are simply unaware of exactly how much money we are spending on groceries and eating out. This week, keep a record of how much you spend on food or use an online program to track your food spending. Consider if there are simple ways you can cut back on the cost of your food, like drinking water when you eat out, sticking to a menu, buying produce in bulk or starting your own herb garden.

▶ **At church:** How can your church address the ever-increasing costs of food? This week consider some ways that members of your church might help each other out. Perhaps a "Costco Club" where bulk quantities of food are split among several people? Or a series of group dinners where a family cooks a meal for a group of church friends and then rotates? Luckily, the cost per meal tends to decrease when more people gather at the table, so eating together can save money and increase the value of the overall meal.

Cauliflower Soup with Carrots and Leeks

Leeks tend to be in season in the winter months, making their cost lower than in the summer. Add other hearty and healthy vegetables to prepare this simple and filling soup.

Prep Time: 20 minutes; **Total Time:** 75 minutes; **Makes 21 servings**
Serving Size: 1 cup
Nutrition Facts (per serving): Calories: 92; Total Fat: 5 g; Saturated Fat: 2 g; Sodium: 189 mg; Carbohydrate: 11 g; Fiber: 2.5 g; Protein: 2 g; Calcium: 46 mg

Ingredients:

2 tablespoons extra-virgin olive oil
3 tablespoons light butter
3 leeks, chopped
1 large head cauliflower, chopped
1 cup carrots, chopped

½ cup yellow or white onions, chopped
3 cloves garlic, minced
8 cups low-sodium vegetable broth
½ cup half and half
Black pepper

Directions:

1. Add oil and butter to a large stockpot at medium-high heat, add oil and butter.
2. Sauté the leeks, cauliflower, carrots, onion and garlic for 10 minutes, stirring occasionally.
3. Pour in the vegetable broth, increase heat to high and bring to boil.
4. Reduce heat to medium, cover and simmer for 45 minutes.
5. Remove the soup from the heat.
6. Pour soup into a blender or food processor and mix until smooth.
7. Season to taste with black pepper.
8. Stir in half and half and serve.

Pasta with Sausage and Pumpkin

Pumpkins aren't just for Halloween! This fall favorite shines as the sauce in this pasta dish. Rich in fiber and flavor, this dish will fill you up on the cheap. If you can't find canned pumpkin, use canned squash.

Prep Time: 10 minutes; **Total Time:** 20 minutes; **Makes 8 servings**
Serving Size: 1 cup
Nutrition Facts (per serving): Calories: 363; Total Fat: 11 g; Saturated Fat: 2 g; Sodium: 412 mg; Carbohydrate: 50 g; Fiber: 7 g; Protein: 18 g; Calcium: 70 mg

Ingredients:

2 tablespoons extra-virgin olive oil
1 lb ground turkey sausage
3 cloves garlic, minced
1 onion, chopped
5 sage leaves, chopped
1½ cups low-sodium vegetable broth
1 cup canned pumpkin

½ cup fat-free half and half
¼ teaspoon ground cinnamon
Dash of salt
1 lb whole-wheat penne pasta
¼ cup Parmesan cheese, shredded
Black pepper

Directions:

1. Add olive oil to a large skillet over medium-high heat.
2. Add sausage, garlic and onions. Cook for about 5 minutes or until sausage is cooked. Drain and set aside.
3. Add sage, broth and pumpkin to pan. Heat and stir for about 5 minutes until sauce comes to a boil.
4. Reduce heat and stir in cooked sausage, garlic, onions, half and half, cinnamon, and salt.
5. Season with pepper to taste. Simmer for about 10 minutes.
6. Serve pasta with sauce and garnish with Parmesan cheese.

Strawberry and Cream Cheese Muffins

Rather than running by the coffee shop, save costs by preparing muffins at home! This tasty muffin gives your day a fresh start with fiber and protein, and helps you to remember to start each day with a healthy breakfast.

Prep Time: 10 minutes; **Total Time:** 35 minutes; **Makes 12 muffins**
Serving Size: 1 muffin
Nutrition Facts (per serving): Calories: 172; Total Fat: 7 g; Saturated Fat: 1.5 g; Sodium: 315 mg; Carbohydrate: 23 g; Fiber: 3 g; Protein: 6 g; Calcium: 107 mg

Ingredients:

4 ounces of light cream cheese, softened
¼ cup lowsugar strawberry preserves
1 cup fresh strawberries, chopped
2¼ cups white, whole-wheat flour
⅓ cup sugar substitute
2 teaspoons baking powder
½ teaspoon baking soda
½ teaspoon salt
2 teaspoons poppy seeds
1¼ cups low-fat buttermilk
¼ cup canola oil
1 egg
2 egg whites
Cooking spray

Directions:

1. Preheat oven to 375 degrees.
2. Combine the cream cheese, preserves and strawberries. Mix well and set aside.
3. Sift the flour, sugar substitute, baking powder, baking soda and salt in a large bowl. Stir in the poppy seeds.
4. In a separate bowl, whisk the buttermilk, oil, egg and egg whites. Add to the flour mixture and stir until all ingredients are moistened.
5. Coat muffin tin with cooking spray. Spoon batter into pan, until each slot is about ⅓ full.
6. Top each with about 1 tablespoon of the strawberry cream cheese mixture. Top with remaining batter.
7. Take a long skewer and swirl cream cheese mixture into the muffin batter.
8. Bake for 25 minutes or until muffins are golden brown on top.

Mexican Lasagna

This filling entrée will make plenty, leaving you room to serve several or save for leftovers. It's also packed with protein and fiber. If you like, consider using ground turkey for a low-fat meat option.

Prep Time: 15 minutes; **Total Time:** 45 minutes; **Makes 8 servings**
Serving Size: 1½ cups
Nutrition Facts (per serving): Calories: 466; Total Fat: 16 g; Saturated Fat: 5 g; Sodium: 510 mg; Carbohydrate: 48 g; Fiber: 9 g; Protein: 34 g

Ingredients:

2 tablespoons extra-virgin olive oil
1 pound ground sirloin
2 tablespoons chili powder
1 teaspoon cumin
1 yellow onion, chopped
1 large tomato, chopped
3 cloves garlic, minced
1 (15-ounce) can black beans, rinsed and drained

1 (15-ounce) can diced tomatoes
1 cup frozen corn
Dash of salt
1 teaspoon onion powder
1 teaspoon garlic powder
16, 4-inch, whole-wheat flour tortillas
2 cups shredded low-fat cheddar cheese
¼ cup green onions, chopped

Directions:

1. Preheat oven to 400 degrees. Heat a large skillet over medium-high heat. Add olive oil. Add sirloin, onion and garlic. Brown the meat until thoroughly cooked, about 5 minutes. Drain and return to skillet. Add chili powder, cumin, chopped tomato, canned tomatoes, black beans, corn, salt, onion powder and garlic powder.
2. Continue cooking over medium high heat for about 5 minutes.
3. Spray a 9x13 inch glass baking dish with cooking spray.
4. Place 4 tortillas halves on bottom of baking dish. Place a third of the sirloin mixture on top followed by ½ cup of the cheese. Repeat with remaining tortillas and sirloin mixture. Sprinkle with remaining ½ cup of cheese.
5. Bake for 15 minutes or until cheese is golden brown.
6. Sprinkle with chopped green onions.

White Bean Dip

This simple dip is easy to make and a great option for a group get-together. Rather than buying a store-bought appetizer, try making this easy snack for yourself and friends to enjoy.

Prep Time: 10 minutes; **Total time:** 15 minutes; **Makes 8 servings**
Serving Size: ¼ cup
Nutrition Facts (per serving): Calories: 77; Total Fat: 2 g; Saturated Fat: 0.5 g; Sodium: 129 mg; Carbohydrate: 13 g; Fiber: 2 g; Protein: 3.5 g

Ingredients:
1 teaspoon olive oil
1 cup onions, chopped
3 cloves garlic, minced
2 tablespoons fresh basil, chopped
2 tablespoons white wine vinegar

1 (15-ounces) can of navy beans, drained and rinsed
8 ounces roasted red bell peppers, drained and chopped

Directions:
1. Heat oil in a medium nonstick skillet over medium heat. Add onion and garlic; sauté 5 minutes or until onions are tender.
2. Combine the onion mixture, basil, vinegar and beans in a food processor. Process until smooth.
3. Stir in bell peppers. Cover with plastic wrap and chill until ready to serve

Spaghetti Squash tossed with Kale and Chickpeas

Try this pasta dish without the pasta! Spaghetti squash is a great, healthy alternative to traditional spaghetti, and one large spaghetti squash can feed several people. We've also made this dish even more non-traditional by adding kale and chickpeas.

Prep Time: 10 minutes; **Total Time:** 25 minutes; **Makes 6 servings**
Serving Size: 1½ cup
Nutrition Facts (per serving): Calories: 223; Total Fat: 11 g; Saturated Fat: 2 g; Sodium: 405 mg; Carbohydrate: 27 g; Fiber: 6 g; Protein: 7 g

Ingredients:

1 spaghetti squash (about 2 lbs)
Cooking spray
¼ cup olive oil
3 cloves garlic
1 bunch of kale, chopped

1 (15-ounce can) chickpeas, no salt added
2 tablespoons pine nuts, toasted
¼ cup Parmesan cheese

Directions:

1. Prepare spaghetti squash by cutting it in half lengthwise and removing the seeds. Place face down in a microwave safe dish and microwave on high for 10 minutes.
2. While squash is cooking, heat oil in large skillet over medium-high heat. Add minced garlic and salt. Cook 2 minutes or until fragrant. Add chopped kale and cook for 1 minute.
3. Remove from heat and add chickpeas.
4. Remove squash from microwave using a fork to scrape out the inside, pulling away from shell in strands, like spaghetti.
5. Place squash in bowl and toss with kale and chickpea mixture.
6. Garnish with toasted pine nuts and Parmesan cheese.

WEEK 5
Honesty: *Knowing What Harms and Heals Us*

MONDAY
Split Pea Soup

TUESDAY
Mediterranean Crustless Quiche

WEDNESDAY
Fettuccini Alfredo with Shrimp

THURSDAY
Sweet Potato Hash with Eggs and Greens

FRIDAY
Grilled Vegetable Pasta

SATURDAY
Spicy Stir-Fry Steak Fajitas

**Fettuccini Alfredo
with Shrimp**
see page 54

**Sweet Potato Hash with
Eggs and Greens**
see page 55

WEEK 5

Honesty: *Knowing What Harms and Heals Us*

Numbers 21:4-9

And the Lord said to Moses, 'Make a poisonous serpent, and set it on a pole; and everyone who is bitten shall look at it and live.' So Moses made a serpent of bronze, and put it upon a pole; and whenever a serpent bit someone, that person would look at the serpent of bronze and live.
     —Numbers 21:8-9

L ent calls us into the places that are dark, upsetting and unjust. It calls us into the wilderness. This is a difficult prospect for many of us who would prefer to not face the wilderness. But we can't do that in Lent. Lent calls us to face up to the things that we have been avoiding and that we pretend are not there. It's our chance to face the wilderness, our chance to be honest and to be healed.

This is what happens in this strange story from Numbers. The Israelites are in the wilderness and speak out against God. God becomes angry and sends snakes to punish them, so the people repent. Yet rather than simply making the snakes disappear, God instructs Moses to make a bronze serpent and raise it high on a pole so that all the people may look at it and be healed. Looking at what is hurting them turns out to be the way they are healed.

As pastor Cornelius Plantinga says, looking at the bronze serpent is like taking a vaccine. By ingesting a small amount of what hurts us, we in fact give our bodies an opportunity fight off the sickness.[4] In Numbers, God makes the Israelites look straight into the face of what is hurting them, and somehow, by looking into the face of the serpent, the Israelites are healed.

This, too, is how we are healed. We have to look at what is hurting us so that we may be healed. We need a truth vaccine, an opportunity to face up to the pain in our lives and find new means of healing. And when it comes to cooking and eating, we have to admit that some of our favorite dishes, and our favorite ways of cooking, are more harmful than healing. In Lent, we have an opportunity to look straight at the cooking practices that are hurting us—and hurting others—and

50

make decisions about how we will do things differently.

There are many daily opportunities to make healthier choices. Perhaps it means cutting back on the butter or eating a smaller piece of pie. Maybe we can challenge ourselves to only buy locally farmed meat, or fruit only when it's in season. Our harmful practices will be different for each of us, yet all of us can make better choices and how and what we eat.

This week we will take this opportunity to prepare some of our favorite dishes, but to do so in a new way. Rather than clinging to cooking practices that are unhealthy, we will look at the challenge of preparing the "classics" in new way. By being honest about the wilderness we face, we can better prepare ourselves for the healing we need.

God in the wilderness, help us to have the courage to face our fears and our limitations. Just as you saved your people in the wilderness, save us from the temptation to pretend that our suffering is not there. Give us the courage to look at the injustice, the pain, and the harmful habits that impede our health and the health of our communities, and restore us to health in You. In Your holy name, Amen.

What To Do:

▶ **At home:** How do our standard cooking practices harm others? This week, consider what kind of produce you buy, or the types and amount of meat you consume. Challenge yourself to learn about where your food comes from, and who produces it. By knowing more about our food, we will be better stewards of the health of our community.

▶ **At church:** Many churches love fried chicken, or some other dish that is almost always unhealthy. Even suggesting that these standard staples might change can provoke anxiety in the church. However, it is important that the church make a consistent commitment to providing healthier foods at coffee hour or church dinners. This week, make a note of the food most often served and think of small ways it could be improved. Providing a sugar-free snack for people with diabetes, or swapping a bowl of fruit for one tray of cookies, can be a step forward.

Split Pea Soup

Split pea soup gets a gourmet makeover by adding turkey sausage and kale. This soup packs nutritional value—full of fiber and protein. Serve this with a small salad and whole-wheat toast for a filling meal.

Prep Time: 5 minutes; **Total Time:** 50 minutes; **Makes 10 servings**
Serving Size: 1 cup
Nutrition Facts (per serving): Calories: 305; Total Fat: 6 g; Sodium: 337 mg; Carbohydrate: 43 g; Fiber: 16 g; Protein: 22 g

Ingredients:

1 tablespoon extra-virgin olive oil
1 large white onion, chopped
3 cloves garlic, chopped
2 large carrots, shredded
1 lb bag green split peas
4 cups low-sodium chicken broth
4 cups kale

8 ounces smoked turkey sausage, sliced thin

Season to taste with:
1 teaspoon onion powder
1 teaspoon garlic powder
½ teaspoon ground black pepper

Directions:

1. Heat oil in a large saucepan over medium-high heat for 30 seconds.
2. Add onion, garlic and carrots. Sauté by mixing continuously and shaking pan for about 3 minutes.
3. Add split peas and broth. Bring mixture to a boil. Lower heat to medium-low and simmer for 30 minutes.
4. Puree mixture in a blender or food processor. Return mixture to saucepan.
5. Bring to a boil and add kale, onion powder, garlic powder, black pepper and turkey sausage.
6. Adjust heat to medium and cook for 10 minutes or until kale is tender.

Mediterranean Quiche

A delicious quiche is almost always filled with heavy cheese and a high-calorie crust. This quiche cuts the calories and packs in the flavors of the Mediterranean. Sun-dried tomatoes and fresh herbs add an extra taste without the fat.

Prep Time: 10 minutes; **Total Time:** 35 minutes; **Makes 6 mini quiches**
Serving Size: 1 mini quiche
Nutrition Facts (per serving): Calories: 131; Total Fat: 9 g; Saturated Fat: 5 g; Sodium: 271 mg; Carbohydrate: 7 g; Fiber: 1 g; Protein: 7 g

Ingredients:

1 tablespoon light butter
½ cup onion, chopped
4 large mushrooms, sliced
1 clove garlic, minced
1 zucchini, chopped
2 ounces sun-dried tomatoes, chopped and drained
2 tablespoons fresh basil, chopped
1 teaspoon fresh thyme, chopped

⅛ teaspoon ground black pepper
Dash of salt
½ cup egg substitute or 2 eggs
¼ teaspoon crushed red pepper flakes
¾ cup fat free half and half
2 ounces gruyere cheese, shredded
3 ounces feta cheese, crumbled
Cooking spray

Directions:

1. Preheat oven to 375 degrees.
2. Melt butter over medium-high heat in a large skillet. Add onion, zucchini, mushrooms and garlic. Cook for about 5 minutes or until vegetables are tender.
3. Add the tomatoes, basil, thyme, salt, pepper and red pepper flakes. Remove skillet from heat and let cool.
4. In a bowl, beat the egg substitute (or eggs) and the half and half with a wire whisk. Add both cheeses.
5. Spoon mixture into a muffin tin coated with cooking spray. Bake for 18 minutes.
6. Remove from oven and let cool for 10 minutes before serving.

Fettuccini Alfredo with Shrimp

A creamy fettuccini alfredo is always a favorite, but this sauce cuts the calories by using fat-free half and half. Adding broccoli to the recipe gives you an extra serving of vegetables.

Prep Time: 10 minutes; **Total Time:** 25 minutes; **Makes 6 servings**
Serving Size: 1½ cups
Nutrition Facts (per serving): Calories: 328;Total Fat: 8 g; Saturated Fat: 3 g; Sodium: 364 mg; Carbohydrate: 38 g; Fiber: 4 g; Protein: 28 g

Ingredients:

½ pound whole-wheat fettuccini pasta
1 tablespoon light butter
1 cup mushrooms, sliced
3 cups fresh broccoli florets, sliced
1 red bell pepper, sliced
1 pound cooked shrimp, peeled and deveined

3 cloves garlic, chopped
½ cup half and half
½ cup fat-free half and half
½ cup Parmesan cheese, shredded
¼ cup flat leaf parsley, chopped
Salt and pepper to taste, if desired

Directions:

1. Cook pasta according to package directions; set aside.
2. In a large nonstick skillet melt butter over medium heat. Add the mushrooms, broccoli, bell pepper and garlic. Cook for about 5 minute or until vegetables are tender.
3. Add the half and half, fat-free half and half, parsley and Parmesan cheese. Cook until sauce is thickened, about 5 minutes, stirring frequently.
4. Stir in cooked shrimp and heat thoroughly.
5. Pour mixture over warm fettuccini noodles.

Sweet Potato Hash with Greens and Eggs

This delicious version of potato hash keeps the home-style taste but uses sweet potatoes to create a much healthier side dish. Cooking the eggs in the hash eliminates the need for extra cooking oil.

Prep Time: 15 minutes; **Total Time:** 60 minutes; **Makes 4 servings**
Serving Size: about ¾ cup
Nutrition Facts (per serving): Calories: 177; Total Fat: 10 g; Saturated Fat: 3 g; Sodium: 313 mg; Carbohydrate: 13 g; Fiber: 3 g; Protein: 10 g

Ingredients:

1 tablespoons olive oil
1 large onion, finely chopped
1 medium sweet potato, chopped
3 cloves garlic, chopped
½ tablespoon water
¼ teaspoon salt

1 teaspoon garlic powder
1 teaspoon onion powder
1 bunch turnip greens, thinly sliced and trimmed
4 large eggs
2 ounces shredded Parmesan cheese

Directions:

1. Heat oil in large skillet over medium heat. Add onions and cook for 5-7 minutes, until onions are translucent.
2. Add chopped sweet potatoes, garlic and water. Cover with a lid and cook for 15 minutes or until sweet potatoes are tender.
3. Remove lid and add salt, garlic powder and onion powder. Add greens, cook for 5 minutes, stirring constantly.
4. Using a spoon, create 4 egg-size wells in the potato mixture. Crack 1 egg into each space.
5. Cover and cook 3 minutes. Remove lid, sprinkle with cheese and then re-cover and cook for 2 more minutes or until egg yolks are lightly set.

Grilled Vegetable Pasta

This easy pasta features fresh vegetables, and the roasted red pepper dressing and seasoning gives this dish some zest.

Prep time: 15 minutes; **Total time:** 20 minutes; **Makes 16 servings**
Serving Size: ¾ cup
Nutrition Facts (per serving): Calories: 175; Total Fat: 3 g; Sodium: 115 mg;
Carbohydrate: 27 g; Fiber: 3 g; Protein: 5 g

Ingredients:

16 ounces cooked whole-wheat penne pasta
½ cup reduced-fat roasted red pepper salad dressing
3 zucchini, sliced thin
3 squash, sliced thin
1 medium-sized eggplant, sliced thin
1 large yellow onion, sliced thin

4 cloves garlic, chopped
⅛ teaspoon crushed red pepper
1 teaspoon hot-and-spicy, salt-free seasoning
½ teaspoon dried basil
½ teaspoon dried oregano
¼ teaspoon dried thyme
1 cup shredded Parmesan cheese

Directions:

1. Place all vegetables in a large bowl, pour dressing over vegetables. Add garlic and all seasonings.
2. Grill vegetables for 5 minutes on your indoor grill.
3. Toss grilled vegetables with pasta in a large bowl, sprinkle with cheese and stir well. Serve warm.

Spicy Stir-Fry Steak Fajitas

Packed with protein, this savory fajita provides the perfect amount of spice. Pair this dish with a small salad garnished with avocado instead of cheese.

Prep Time: 10 minutes; **Total Time:** 50 minutes (30 minutes for marinating)
Makes 6 servings
Serving Size: 1 fajita
Nutrition Facts (per serving): Calories: 241; Total Fat: 6 g; Saturated Fat: 2 g; Sodium: 332 mg; Carbohydrate: 26 g; Fiber: 4 g; Protein: 20 g

Ingredients for Fajita Marinade:

1 teaspoon grated lime zest
¼ cup fresh lime juice
1 tablespoon balsamic vinegar
2 cloves garlic, minced
Dash of sea salt
½ teaspoon ground black pepper
¼ teaspoon ground cumin

1 large onion, sliced thin
1 medium red bell pepper, sliced thin
1 medium green bell pepper, sliced thin
1 jalapeno pepper, chopped
6 whole-wheat flour tortillas
Dash of hot sauce
1 cup plain, non-fat yogurt or Greek yogurt

Ingredients for Fajita Filling:

1 lb sirloin, trimmed of fat
2 teaspoons canola oil

Directions:

1. Combine lime zest, lime juice, balsamic vinegar, garlic, sea salt, pepper, and cumin in a small bowl.
2. Thinly slice meat across the grain and marinate in the bowl of ingredients above.
3. Cover and refrigerate for about 30 minutes.
4. Combine stir-fry oil, peppers, meat, and onions in a nonstick skillet over medium-high heat for about 5 minutes or until meat is cooked
5. Warm tortillas as desired. Fill each with the mixture of marinated meat, peppers, and onions.
6. Add hot sauce and yogurt as desired.
7. Roll tortillas and serve.

WEEK 6
Humility: *Being Open to New Ideas*

MONDAY
Cashew Ginger Chicken Soup

TUESDAY
Eggplant Quesadilla

WEDNESDAY
Peach and Walnut Barley Salad

THURSDAY
*Spinach Basil Hummus and
Whole-Wheat Herb Crackers*

FRIDAY
Roasted Vegetable Tart

SATURDAY
Sesame Noodle Salad Bowl

Peach and Walnut
Barley Salad
see page 64

Roasted Vegetable Tart
see page 66

Humility: *Being Open to New Ideas*
Psalm 51

Purge me with hyssop, and I shall be clean; wash me, and I shall be whiter than snow.
  —Psalm 51:7

A traveler with a strong nose can find the spices and smells of the Bible in the middle of urban Amsterdam. The Bijbels Museum, or Bible Museum, is a three-story building with replicas of the Second Temple and thousands of Bibles from all over the world. Its most interesting feature, however, is the smelling huts. Two plant conservatories flank the outside gardens and invite you to smell and touch spices often mentioned in the Bible—frankincense, henna, nard and hyssop.

With its graying leaves, the hyssop plant itself is not much to look at, and its proclivity to grow in the cracks of the rock make it much less valuable than other spices. Yet in the Biblical period, hyssop was widely available and used for seasoning, medicine, and kindling. It is known as a humble and modest plant, which is perhaps why the psalmist asks to be washed clean by it. The psalmist does not pray for an extravagant anointing, but rather to be made clean and pure by the leaves of humility.

In the kitchen and at the table, humility is an important virtue. Many of us will have pre-conceived notions about how we like to cook, and what we like to eat. We might prefer to stick with "the way we've always done it" and know for a fact that we don't like a certain food. But cooking and enjoying healthy foods means that we must have a new outlook and a new attitude. We have to be willing to concede that some of our preferences are unhealthy, and that there may be new opportunities at the table.

This week we explore foods and tastes that may be new to us. Rather than approaching them with skepticism, try to have an open outlook and push yourself to try new things that you might otherwise avoid. Even if we figure out that we don't like a dish, approaching the kitchen with humility means that we can find unexpected ways to be made whole.

God of new life, wash us with the leaves of the hyssop and usher us into a new way of being. Help us to have an open mind and to challenge ourselves in the kitchen, at the table, and in our daily lives. Give us comfort when we fail, and create a new heart within us, each and every day. In Your holy name, Amen.

What to do:

▶ **At home:** Cooking is not always something that comes easy to us. There are special techniques and tools that can seem complicated or intimidating. This week, pick a cooking technique that you have yet to master and make a plan for tackling it.

▶ **At church:** Many of our food preferences are formed when we are young. We grow up thinking that Brussels sprouts and broccoli are yucky, and reward our children with chicken fingers and pizza. Try to inspire a love of new foods among the children in your church by holding a fun tasting session. Use the Church Health Center's *Alphabet Appetite* as a means of exploring new foods for children.

Cashew Ginger-Chicken Soup

Unconventional flavors like ginger, kale and cashews form this creative soup. Use any remaining cashew butter to add taste to a piece of toasted whole-grain bread.

Prep Time: 15 minutes ; **Total Time:** 40 minutes; **Makes 8 servings**
Serving Size: 1 cup
Nutrition Facts (per serving): Calories: 196; Total Fat: 11 g; Saturated Fat: 2 g; Sodium: 533 mg; Carbohydrate: 16 g; Fiber: 2 g; Protein: 10 g

Ingredients:

6 cups low-sodium chicken broth
1 large onion, in peeled strips
2 cloves garlic, chopped
1 tablespoon fresh ginger, finely chopped
1 large sweet potato, chopped
1 bunch of kale leaves, chopped

1 large, raw chicken breast (6 ounces), cubed
½ cup cashew butter
1 teaspoon fresh lime juice (1 half of a lime)
2 limes, cut into 4 wedges
½ teaspoon red pepper flakes

Directions:

1. Bring chicken broth to boil in large pot.
2. Add onions, garlic, ginger and chicken.
3. Lower heat and simmer at just below boiling point over medium heat for 10 minutes.
4. Add sweet potatoes and cook for an additional 10 minutes.
5. Add kale and spices and cook for 3 minutes or until kale is slightly wilted and sweet potatoes are soft.
6. Whisk together lime juice and cashew butter in small bowl. Add cashew mixture to soup.
7. Ladle into six bowls and serve with lime wedge.

Eggplant Quesadilla

Don't be intimidated by eggplant! When choosing an eggplant, select ones that are firm and heavy for their size. To test ripeness, gently press the skin with the pad of your thumb. It should spring back—if the indent stays, it is not ripe.

Prep Time: 15 minutes; **Total Time:** 30-45 minutes; **Makes 4 servings**
Serving Size: 1 quesadilla
Nutrition Facts (per serving): Calories: 262; Total Fat: 8 g; Saturated Fat: 2 g; Sodium: 347 mg; Carbohydrate: 36 g; Fiber: 6 g; Protein: 12 g

Ingredients:

2 eggplants
4 12-inch whole-wheat tortillas
8 ounces low-fat, low-sodium shredded Jack cheese

1 bunch fresh basil, chopped
2-3 tomatoes, chopped
1 cup sliced roasted peppers, reserve oil for grilling eggplant

Directions:

1. If using a grill, heat the grill. Slice eggplant into ½ inch slices.
2. Brush slices with oil from roasted peppers.
3. If you are using a grill, grill eggplant, basting occasionally with more roasted pepper oil until slices are very soft. If using a grill pan, cook over medium-high heat and cook each side about 5-7 minutes or until tender when stuck with a fork. If you do not have a grill pan, you can roast the eggplant in a 425 degree oven for 20-25 minutes or until tender when stuck with a fork.
4. Layer cheese, basil, eggplant, tomatoes and peppers inside a tortilla.
5. Fold tortilla in half.
6. Bake tortilla (400 degrees) or cook on a hot griddle until center is hot and outside is brown and crisp.

Peach and Walnut Barley Salad

Peaches and goat cheese create a savory and sweet complement to one another in this healthy barley salad. This flavorful side dish is packed with surprising bursts of flavor and is a great side dish or snack. For dinner, try pairing it with a piece of fish, whole-grain roll and a fresh salad.

Prep Time: 10 minutes; **Total Time:** 30 minutes; **Makes 8 servings**
Serving Size: ½ cup
Nutrition Facts (per serving): Calories: 139; Total Fat: 4 g; Saturated Fat: 1 g; Sodium: 162 mg; Carbohydrate: 22 g; Fiber: 5 g; Protein: 4 g

Ingredients:

1 cup quick-cooking barley
1 cup parsley leaves, finely chopped
¼ cup walnut pieces, chopped
1 peach, peeled, pitted and diced
½ cup red bell pepper, diced
1 tablespoon extra-virgin olive oil

2 tablespoons lime juice (about 2 limes)
1 orange, juiced
½ teaspoon chili powder
¼ teaspoon salt
¼ cup low-fat goat cheese, crumbled

Directions:

1. Cook barley according to package directions, omitting salt.
2. Drain remaining liquid from barley. Stir in parsley, walnuts, peach and pepper.
3. In a small bowl, combine oil, lime juice, orange juice, chili powder and salt. Pour over barley mixture and toss together.
4. Crumble goat cheese over top and serve.

Spinach Basil Hummus with Whole-wheat Herb Crackers

Many of us are familiar with hummus and crackers but have never made them from scratch! Rather than buying hummus and salty crackers, try to make them at home. Double the hummus recipe or set aside a ½ cup of hummus to use for tomorrow's Roasted Vegetable Tart.

Spinach Basil Hummus:

Prep Time: 5 minutes; **Total Time:** 10 minutes; **Makes 2 cups (16 servings)**
Serving Size: 2 tablespoons
Nutrition Facts (per serving): Calories: 54; Total Fat: 4 g; Saturated Fat: 1 g; Sodium: 151 mg; Carbohydrate: 4 g; Fiber: 1 g; Protein: 2 g

Ingredients:
1 (15 ounce) can chickpeas, reduced sodium
¼ cup tahini
2 tablespoons olive oil
Juice of 1 lemon
1 teaspoon salt
½ teaspoon black pepper
½ cup water
1 garlic clove
½ cup fresh basil
1 cup fresh spinach

Directions:
1. Drain and rinse chickpeas.
2. Add all ingredients into food processor and process until smooth. If mixture is too thick add 1 tablespoon water and process again.

Whole-wheat Herb Crackers:

Prep Time: 10 minutes; **Total Time:** 35 minutes; **Makes 36 crackers (6 Servings)**
Serving Size: 6 crackers
Nutrition Facts (per serving): Calories: 85; Total Fat: 2 g; Saturated Fat: 0 g; Sodium: 222 mg; Carbohydrate: 16 g; Fiber: 3 g; Protein: 3 g

Ingredients:
1 cup white, whole-wheat flour
2 tablespoons ground flaxseed
⅛ teaspoon baking soda
¾ teaspoon salt
1 teaspoon dried rosemary
1 teaspoon dried sage
½ teaspoon olive oil
2 cloves garlic, minced
¼ cup water (or more as needed)

Directions:
1. Preheat oven to 350 degrees.
2. Combine dry ingredients in large bowl and mix until well combined.
3. Add olive oil, garlic and water, and mix until dough forms.
4. Sandwich the dough between two sheets of parchment paper and roll out using a rolling pin, making dough as thin as possible, about ⅛ inch thick.
5. Cut into 1x1 inch squares, using a fork poke holes into each cracker to prevent them from puffing.
6. Bake for 15-20 minutes or until the edges are starting to brown.

Roasted Vegetable Tart

By adding tons of vegetables together in this dish, we can feel satisfied – with our meal and in our stomachs!

Prep Time: 15 minutes; Total Time: 45 minutes; **Makes 16 square slices**
Serving Size: 1 square
Nutrition Facts (per serving): Calories: 153; Total Fat: 9.5 g; Saturated Fat: 1 g; Sodium: 115 mg; Carbohydrate: 15 g; Fiber: 4 g; Protein: 3 g

Crust Ingredients:
2 cups white whole-wheat flour
½ cup olive oil
5½ tablespoons club soda, chilled
½ teaspoon salt
½ teaspoon Italian seasoning
Fresh cracked black pepper

Filling Ingredients:
1 medium onion, sliced
1 medium tomato, sliced

2 medium zucchini, sliced
2 small eggplant, sliced
1 medium red bell pepper, sliced
2 garlic cloves, chopped
2 teaspoons olive oil
¼ teaspoon salt
Cooking spray
Parchment Paper
½ cup Spinach Basil Spread (from yesterday)

Directions for Assembling Tart:
1. Allow crust to cool.
2. Spread ¼ cup of basil hummus spread on each tart.
3. Arrange roasted vegetables on the top of the tart.
4. Sprinkle with sea salt, black pepper and cooking spray.
5. Bake tart in oven for 2 minutes or just until warm at 350 degrees.

Directions for Vegetables:
1. Place onion, tomato, zucchini, eggplant, and bell pepper in gallon size plastic bag.
2. Add olive oil, cloves and salt. Seal bag and shake until all vegetables are well coated.
3. Place vegetables on foil lined cookie sheet and roast at 400 degrees for 25 minutes.

Directions for Crust:
1. In a medium bowl, whisk together flour, salt, black pepper and Italian seasoning, set aside.
2. In a separate small bowl, whisk together oil and club soda for about 2 minutes until creamy.
3. Pour oil mixture (small bowl) over flour mixture (large bowl) and stir together with a fork until doughy.
4. Divided dough into two equal parts and roll gently between two sheets of parchment paper, in a single direction. Make sure that crusts are of similar size, about ½ inch thick flat ovals.
5. Remove the top parchment paper. Trim the edges of the dough as desired and prick the crust with a fork.
6. Bake the crust on parchment paper at 400 degrees for 12 minutes.

Sesame Noodle Salad Bowl

Cooking Asian food doesn't have to be complicated! This noodle salad is easy to make and keeps you from calling for take-out.

Prep Time: 15 minutes; **Total Time:** 10 minutes ; **Makes 4 servings**
Serving Size: 1¼ cups
Nutrition Facts (per serving): Calories: 225; Total Fat: 11 g; Saturated Fat: 1 g; Sodium: 278 mg; Carbohydrate: 27 g; Fiber: 4.5 g; Protein: 7 g; Calcium: 38 mg

Ingredients for the Dressing:

¼ cup fresh squeezed lime juice
2 tablespoons low-sodium soy sauce
1 tablespoon dark brown sugar
1 tablespoon water
1 tablespoon sesame oil
1 tablespoon red curry paste
1 tablespoon grated fresh ginger
1 tablespoon canola oil
Salt and pepper to taste

Ingredients for the Salad:

8 ounces cooked whole-wheat spaghetti, drained and rinsed under cold water
2 cups fresh bean spouts
2 cups fresh baby spinach leaves, chopped
1 large red bell pepper, sliced thin
¼ cup green onions, chopped
¼ cup fresh cilantro, chopped
1 ounce peanuts, finely chopped

Directions:

1. To prepare the dressing, combine all dressing ingredients in a large metal bowl, whisk until blended well, set aside.
2. To prepare salad, combine all salad ingredients. Pour dressing over pasta mixture and mix well.
3. Chill in refrigerator for at least 30 minuets. Sprinkle with peanuts.

WEEK 7
Diversity: *Enjoying the Food of the World*

MONDAY
Quick Three-Bean Chili

TUESDAY
Eggplant Dip and Cumin Crisps

WEDNESDAY
Cashew Crusted Tilapia with Mango

THURSDAY
Lemon Mushroom Kale

FRIDAY
Home-style Biscuits

SATURDAY
Rosemary Chicken

Eggplant Dip and
Cumin Crisps
see page 73

Lemon Mushroom Kale
see page 75

Diversity: *Enjoying the Food of the World*

Philippians 2:5-11

Let the same mind be in you that was in Christ Jesus.
—Philippians 2:5

The birthplace of Jesus is not a manger but a cave. In the Church of the Nativity in Bethlehem, the site of Jesus' birth is housed in a poorly lit grotto, an underground cave located beneath the basilica. The grotto is very small, with just a few seats for people to sit and pray, and the site of Jesus' birth is marked on the floor with a silver star.

Naturally, Christians from all over the world travel to the Church of the Nativity to visit this sacred site. Orthodox Christians from Eastern Europe meet up with Baptists from the southern United States and Roman Catholics from Central America, and all of them squeeze into this small grotto to sit next to each other and pray. The effect of all these Christians gathered together, with different languages, different customs and even different beliefs, can be both inspiring and troubling. Even among the priests who maintain the Church, differences can be a source of violence, and inter-church squabbles have provoked fighting even in the recent past.[5] When you encounter such wide difference, it can be difficult to remember that all of these people are Christians who profess Jesus Christ is Lord—even if they disagree about how you do that.

Paul is not unacquainted with the blessings and problems of very different people coming together in Christ. The Roman Empire in which he ministered was diverse and complicated, and the Church brought together people of different languages and customs, just as it does today. Paul's letter to the church in Philippi urges the believers to be of a same mind in Christ, looking out for the interests of others rather than the interests of ourselves or our immediate circle of friends. Even in the midst of extreme difference, Paul encourages us to remember that Jesus came to us in human form, so that all humanity—not just the parts of humanity that look or talk like us—will bow before the name of Jesus.

During this Holy Week, we will remember the very great diversity of Christianity by exploring the foods and traditions of different cultures. Just as Jesus challenged himself and the authorities by leaving the quiet of Galilee and going into Jerusalem, the heart of the nation, we will leave the comfort of our homes to travel to different places through the food of Holy Week. Especially this week, we will celebrate that God does not reside in only one place or another but rather, that the sacrifice and saving grace of Jesus is celebrated in all of creation.

God of every time and place, walk with us in this Holiest of Weeks. Help us to remember that your saving grace is in every corner of creation: the quiet, the dirty, the restful and the restless. Connect us to Christians all over your world, giving us security in the midst of pain and friendship in the middle of isolation. Let us remember that with each passing day, we strive to live into the sacrificing love that you offer to us in these, our most holy days. Amen.

What to do:

▶ **At home:** Holy Week can be a time for both introspection and community. This week, try to carve out some extra time to spend at church. If your church has a daily worship service, or special services on Holy Thursday, Good Friday or Easter Saturday, try to attend one or several of the services that you rarely go to. If your church or tradition does not typically have extra services during Holy Week, gather together a small group of friends for a special Holy Week prayer session.

▶ **At church:** Holy or Maundy Thursday is traditionally the time when churches celebration Holy Communion or the Eucharist. Depending on your liturgical tradition, explore how you might incorporate your learnings from *Seasoning Lent* in your communion service. If you use loaves of bread, make sure that they are locally made and that you provide a gluten-free option. Or think about gathering the community around the table for a special blessing. While our traditions may differ, Jesus certainly gathered his friends around the table at this special meal. Explore how you might invite that same spirit into your Thursday service.

Quick Three-Bean Chili

Fanesca is the traditional soup of Ecuador and is typically served during Holy Week. Its preparations vary from region to region but its twelve different kinds of beans are meant to represent the twelve apostles. This week we will prepare Quick Three-Bean Chili to celebrate this traditional Holy Week food of Ecuador and remember the apostles.

Prep Time: 15 minutes; **Total Time:** 30 minutes; **Makes 6 servings**
Serving Size: 1⅓ cup
Nutrition Facts (per serving): Calories: 249; Total Fat: 4 g; Saturated Fat: 1 g; Sodium: 181 mg; Carbohydrate: 41 g; Fiber: 14 g; Protein: 14 g

Ingredients:

2 teaspoons canola oil
1½ cup onion and bell pepper mix, frozen and pre-chopped
1(8 ounces)package of sliced mushrooms
2 cloves garlic
¾ cup water
2 tablespoons tomato paste
2 teaspoons chili powder
2 teaspoons cumin
¼ teaspoon black pepper
½ teaspoon red pepper flakes
1(15 ounce) can navy beans, rinsed and drained

1 (15 ounce) can red kidney beans, rinsed and drained
1 (15 ounce) can black beans, rinsed and drained
1 (14 ounce) can low-sodium vegetable broth
1 (14 ounce) can no-salt-added diced tomatoes, undrained
1 tablespoon yellow cornmeal
6 tablespoons sour cream, reduced fat (or low-fat yogurt)

Directions:

1. Heat oil in large saucepan over medium-high heat.
2. Add onion, bell pepper, mushrooms, and garlic to pan. Cook 3 minutes.
3. Add water and the next 10 ingredients: tomato paste, chili powder, cumin, black pepper, red pepper flakes, navy beans, kidney beans, black beans, vegetable broth, and diced tomatoes.
4. Bring to a boil. Reduce heat, and simmer for 10 minutes.
5. Stir in cornmeal and cook for a few minutes longer.

Eggplant Dip and Cumin Crisps

Many Christian Filipinos often refrain from eating meat during Lent. Tortang talong is an eggplant omelette popular among many Filipinos. This week we will prepare eggplant dip as a way of celebrating the traditions and cuisine of the Philippines.

Prep Time: 15 minutes; **Total Time:** 50 minutes; **Makes 6 servings**
Serving Size: ⅓ cup dip and 5 pita wedges
Nutrition Facts (per serving): Calories: 168; Total Fat: 10 g; Saturated Fat: 1 g; Sodium: 181 mg; Carbohydrates: 19 g; Fiber: 5 g; Protein: 4 g

Ingredients for Eggplant Dip:

1 tablespoon extra-virgin olive oil
1 large eggplant
1 cup mushrooms, sliced thin
1 green bell pepper, seeded and diced
1 small yellow onion, diced
3 cloves garlic, minced
1 lemon, juiced
Dash of salt
Freshly ground black pepper to taste, about ¼ teaspoon
¼ cup pine nuts
5 jumbo black olives, sliced thin
2 tablespoons flat leaf parsley, chopped

Ingredients for Cumin Crisps:

4 4-inch whole-wheat pitas, split in half and cut into 4 wedges
1 tablespoon extra-virgin olive oil
2 teaspoons cumin
1 teaspoon onion powder
1 teaspoon garlic powder
2 teaspoons paprika
Dash of salt

Directions for the Eggplant Dip:

1. Preheat oven to 450 degrees. Place the eggplant on a cookie sheet lined with foil and sprayed with cooking spray. Prick the skin of the eggplant several times with a fork. Bake for 40 minutes. Remove from oven and set aside to cool.
2. In a nonstick skillet heated to medium high heat add the olive oil. Stir in the mushrooms, green bell peppers, onion and garlic. Sauté for about 5 minutes. Set aside.
3. Slice the eggplant in half lengthwise and scoop out the flesh of the eggplant and place in a food processor. Discard skin of the eggplant. Add the sautéed vegetables, lemon juice, salt and pepper to food processor. Process until smooth. Put the mixture into a serving bowl.
4. Place the pine nuts on a small cookie sheet and bake until golden, about 4 minutes.
5. Place pine nuts and sliced black olives over the eggplant dip. Sprinkle with parsley.

For the Cumin Criisps:

1. Preheat oven to 400 degrees. Place pita wedges on a cookie sheet. Brush with olive oil.
2. In a small bowl, stir the cumin, onion powder, garlic powder, paprika and salt.
3. Sprinkle over the pita wedges. Bake for 6 minutes.

Cashew Crusted Tilapia with Mango

In Spanish, Holy Week is known as Semana Santa. Similar to other countries, many Spanish cooks prepare dishes with fish and vegetables during Holy Week. Today we will make cashew crusted tilapia to remember the different ways that the people of Spain honor Lent.

Prep Time: 10 minutes; **Total Time:** 20 minutes; **Makes 4 servings**
Serving Size: 1 fish fillet with ½ cup salsa
Nutrition Facts (per serving): Calories: 315; Total Fat: 13 g; Saturated Fat: 2 g; Sodium: 190 mg; Carbohydrate: 18 g; Fiber: 2 g; Protein: 29 g; Calcium: 59 mg

Ingredients:

1 large mango, chopped
1 large tomato, seeded and chopped
¼ cup yellow onion, chopped fine
¼ cup fresh cilantro, chopped fine
1 lime, juiced and zested
Dash of salt
Pepper to taste

3 egg whites
¼ cup cashews, crushed fine
¼ cup yellow cornmeal
4 4-ounce tilapia fillets
1 teaspoon olive oil
1 teaspoon light butter

Directions:

1. In a medium-sized bowl, combine the mango, tomatoes, onion, cilantro, lime juice, lime zest, salt and pepper. Set aside.
2. Place egg white in another bowl.
3. Mix cashews and cornmeal in another bowl.
4. Coat with egg whites, then cashew mixture. Place coated fish on a clean plate.
5. Heat a large nonstick skillet to medium-high heat. Add olive oil and butter. Add filets and cook for about 3 minutes on each side.
6. Serve with mango salsa on top.

Lemon Mushroom Kale

In Germany, Austria and other countries, Holy Thursday is sometimes called Gründonnerstag, which means Green Thursday. The word "grün" derives from the ancient German word "greinen," which means "to cry or to moan," and meals on Holy Thursday often feature green vegetables, parsley and chives. Today we will prepare Lemon Mushroom Kale to remember Green Thursday.

Prep Time: 15 minutes; **Total Time:** 50 minutes; **Makes 4 servings**
Serving Size: about 1½ cups
Nutrition Facts (per serving): Calories: 124; Total Fat: 6 g; Saturated Fat: 1 g; Sodium: 362 mg; Carbohydrate: 19 g; Fiber: 3 g; Protein: 4 g

Ingredients:
1 tablespoon olive oil
1 bunch of kale, stemmed and chopped
1 teaspoon salt
½ teaspoon black pepper
1 tablespoon lemon juice
¼ cup low sodium vegetable broth
1 cup chopped mushrooms
⅓ cup dried cranberries
1 tablespoon pine nuts, toasted

Directions:
1. Heat oil in large saucepan over medium heat.
2. Add in mushrooms, salt and pepper. Cook for 2-3 minutes, stirring constantly.
3. Add kale and allow it to start to wilt. Squeeze in lemon juice and pour vegetable broth over kale.
4. Once kale has decreased in size by half, toss in cranberries and toasted pine nuts and serve warm.

Home-style Biscuits

Hot-cross buns are a traditional food of Good Friday in the United Kingdom and other countries. There are many traditions and stories about how hot-cross buns came to be associated with Good Friday. One tradition says that sharing a hot-cross bun with a friend on Good Friday will bring you good luck. Whether or not good luck comes your way, sharing this sweet treat is a good way to keep your calories under control. Today we will make this home-style biscuits. Don't forget to make a cross on the top of the dough!

Prep time: 5 minutes; **Total time:** 20 minutes; **Makes 15 biscuits**
Serving Size: 1 biscuit
Nutrition Facts (per serving): Calories: 95; Total Fat: 3 g; Sodium: 50 mg; Carbohydrate: 14 g; Fiber: 1 g; Protein: 2 g

Ingredients:

1 cup all-purpose flour
1 cup whole-wheat flour
2 teaspoons baking powder
¼ teaspoon baking soda
¼ teaspoon salt

2 tablespoons sugar
⅔ cup low fat buttermilk
3 tablespoons plus 1 teaspoon canola oil

Directions:

1. Preheat oven to 450 degrees. In a medium bowl, combine the flour, baking powder, baking soda, salt and sugar.
2. In a small bowl, stir together buttermilk and oil.
3. Pour over flour mixture and stir well.
4. On a floured surface, knead dough gently for 12 strokes.
5. Roll dough into a ¾ inch thickness.
6. Cut with a 2-inch biscuit or cookie cutter, dipping cutter in flour between cuts.
7. Place biscuits on an ungreased baking sheet.
8. Bake for 12 minutes or until golden brown.

Rosemary Chicken

On this 40th day of Lent, we remember all of the events that have led up to this day. We remember the pain of Good Friday, but also remember the joy of Easter Sunday that is yet to come. The herb rosemary is traditionally known as the herb of remembrance, so on this day we will prepare Rosemary Chicken as a way of remembering the many steps we have traveled over our Lenten journey.

Prep Time: 5 minutes; **Total Time:** 30 minutes; **Makes 6 servings**
Serving Size: 1 chicken breast
Nutrition Facts (per serving): Calories: 147; Fat: 2 g; Cholesterol: 68 mg; Sodium: 79 mg; Carbohydrates: 3.7 g; Protein: 27 g

Ingredients:
6 skinless, boneless chicken breasts
1 cup fresh rosemary, leaves trimmed
from stalk
1 tablespoon lemon juice
Salt
Pepper

Directions:
1. Preheat oven to 375 degrees.
2. Place the chicken breasts in a 9x13 baking dish. Cover chicken breasts with rosemary, lemon juice, salt and pepper.
3. Bake for 25 minutes or until done and juices run clear.

Easter Sunday

Grace: *Celebrating the Love of God*
1 Corinthians 15:1-11

But by the grace of God I am what I am, and his grace toward me has not been in vain. On the contrary, I worked harder than any of them—though it was not I, but the grace of God that is with me.
—1 Corinthians 15:10

Paul tells us that when we can push ourselves into areas of great challenge, we can be confident in God's grace. This is most true on Easter Sunday! On this day, we celebrate that God has conquered every challenge we might ever face, even death. Because of God's all-encompassing love and power, we are assured that our efforts are not in vain. The grace of God reaches into each and every part of our lives, redeeming and renewing us.

Throughout Lent, we have challenged ourselves to cook new meals and explore new tastes. We have addressed the cost of eating healthy, faced the wilderness of change, sacrificed for our community and brought humility to the kitchen. Through our Lenten practice, we have prepared ourselves for a healthier and happier Easter Sunday. And if we have made it this far, we must rejoice in the knowledge that God has been with us on the journey!

Today we invite you to explore some of your favorite dishes from *Seasoning Lent* and to share with others the gracious lessons you have learned along your Lenten journey. Perhaps you want to invite your entire family over to enjoy the food, or perhaps you want to share it with one special friend. The size and number of the feast is not the important part of this practice; the important element is to share with others the good news of your success over the last several weeks and enjoy the healthy, delicious foods you have practiced.

God of glory, we come to you on this Easter Day with healthy, hopeful hearts. Just as you rose from the grave, transforming the world and showing us the ways of God's love, help us to celebrate the ways that we have struggled through these last 40 days and yet emerged from our tombs. Sit with us at this table and inspire in us the simple joy of eating together and sharing in the feast of your Resurrection table. In Your holy name, Amen.

▶ **At home:** Prepare a healthy Easter Sunday meal for friends and family using the recipes from *Seasoning Lent*. Choose your favorite items or use this meal suggestion:

Appetizer: Eggplant Caviar and Cumin Crisps
Main Dish: Rosemary Chicken
Side Dishes: Carrot Souffle, Lemon Green Beans,
Mediterranean Crustless Quiche, Home-style biscuits
Dessert: Strawberry and Cream Cheese Muffins

▶ **At church:** Offer a prayer of thanksgiving or blessing to the participants in *Seasoning Lent*. Try to find a way to acknowledge the sacrifices the community has made over the last 40 days and celebrate that in worship.

Recipe List

Week 1
Change: What You Eat Matters
Monday: Gouda Macaroni and Cheese
Tuesday: The Best Chili
Wednesday: Baked Pretzels
Thursday: Kale Chips
Friday: Pumpkin Quesadillas with Cranberry Orange
    Salsa
Saturday: Steamed Broccoli

Week 2
Water: What You Drink Matters
Monday: White Bean Soup
Tuesday: Braised Asparagus
Wednesday: Stuffed Apples
Thursday: Spicy Thai Coconut Shrimp
Friday: Penne Pasta with Spinach
Saturday: Poppy Seed Chicken Casserole

Week 3
Sacrifice: Making the Most of our Resources
Monday: Spicy Tomato Soup
Tuesday: Oven-Fried Chicken
Wednesday: Lemon Green Beans
Thursday: Carrot Soufflé
Friday: Mediterranean Roasted Broccoli and
    Tomatoes
Saturday: Tilapia in a Bag

Week 4
Value: Cost v. Quality
Monday: Cauliflower Soup with Carrots and Leeks
Tuesday: Penne Pasta with Pumpkin and Sausage
Wednesday: Strawberry and Cream Cheese Muffins
Thursday: Mexican Lasagna
Friday: White Bean Dip
Saturday: Spaghetti Squash with Kale and Chickpeas

Week 5
Honesty: Knowing what Harms and Heals Us
Monday: Split Pea Soup
Tuesday: Mediterranean Crustless Quiche
Wednesday: Fettuccini Alfredo with Shrimp
Thursday: Sweet Potato Hash with Eggs and Greens
Friday: Grilled Vegetable Pasta
Saturday: Spicy Stir-Fry Steak Fajitas

Week 6
Humility: Being Open to New Ideas
Monday: Cashew Ginger Chicken Soup
Tuesday: Eggplant Quesadilla
Wednesday: Peach and Walnut Barley Salad
Thursday: Spinach Basil Hummus and Whole-Wheat
    Herb Crackers
Friday: Roasted Vegetable Tart
Saturday: Sesame Noodle Salad Bowl

Week 7
Diversity: Enjoying the Food of the World
Monday: Quick Three-Bean Chili
Tuesday: Eggplant Dip and Cumin Crisps
Wednesday: Cashew Crusted Tilapia with Mango
Thursday: Lemon Mushroom Kale
Friday: Home-style Biscuits
Saturday: Rosemary Chicken

Notes

[1] *Be Diligent: Serving Others as You Walk With the Master Servant* by Warren W. Wiersbe. Published by David C. Cook., 1987. p. 107

[2] "Water" by Wendell Berry. *From Farming: A Handbook*. Published by Harcourt Press, 1970.

[3] "Is Junk Food Really Cheaper?" by Mark Bittman. From *The New York Times*, September 24, 2011.

[4] "Christ, the Snake" by Cornelius Plantinga. *Perspectives*, Volumes 6-8. Reformed Church in America. Published by Reformed Church Press, 1991.

[5] "Police storm Church of the Nativity to break up brawling priests," by Enas Muthaffar and Kevin Flower. From CNN, December 28, 2011.